SCOTLAND THROUGH HER
COUNTRY DANCES

To
the memory
of
Jean C. Milligan

SCOTLAND

THROUGH

HER

COUNTRY

DANCES

(2ND EDITION)

GEORGE S. EMMERSON

GALT HOUSE
565 Kininvie Dr.
London, Ont.
Canada
N6G 1P1

GEORGE EMMERSON © 1981

ISBN 0-9690653-0-2

First Published 1967
Second Edition 1981

Made and printed in Canada
by Skinner Printing, Petrolia, Ontario
for Galt House

CONTENTS

EIGHTEENTH CENTURY SCOTLAND

INTRODUCTION

A glance at the titles of Scottish Country Dances and their tunes cannot fail to stimulate myriad associations in the minds of those familiar with Scotland's song and story, and equally myriad curiosities in the minds of those who are familiar only with the dances themselves. The social life, the beauty of the countryside; the old issues and causes which ennobled and enfeebled; the celebrated personalities who enlivened Court and causey; the forms of dress, of custom, of conduct; the earthiness, the pathos, the sublimity and comedy of Scottish life; all of these and much more find allusion in these titles.

Until very recently, Country Dances took the titles of their tunes. Only occasionally, however, in the older dances, can one perceive in their figures any relationship to the ideas suggested by their titles. Even then, one cannot be sure that the relationship is not fortuitous, although it seems very strong in a very few instances, such as *The Machine Without Horses* and *The Duchess of Athole's Slipper*, as published by the R.S.C.D.S.

Among the eighteenth and nineteenth century collections one often finds several different figures set to the same tune and consequently bearing the same name. Sometimes, too, a particular set of figures has been attached to different tunes and hence appears under different names. This explains the proliferation of alternative titles to the dances first collected and published by the R.S.C.D.S. That Society, however, has often deemed it necessary, or desirable, to edit the dances; in a few cases to such a degree that very little but the title — or one of the titles — remains of the original. This has shocked some of those who placed emphasis on the Society's antiquarian role and who therefore accused the Society of misleading its devotees. But those who placed emphasis on the Society's practical goal of having Scotland dance again to its Country Dances were concerned with making the dances comfortably danceable. Sometimes the interpretation of an old figure gave trouble and, in earlier centuries, the execution and technique were somewhat arbitrary in any case. Unlike the English Folk Dance Society, the R.S.C.D.S. has only secondary interest in the antiquarian side of its purpose; but it has restored the dances and promoted their performance by thousands of people throughout the world.

The titles of the old dances or the old titles of the dances have special meaning for all interested in Scotland and Scottish lore. Hence this book.

ACKNOWLEDGEMENTS

This book would not have come into being had the work of the Royal Scottish Country Dance Society not given it occasion. The founders of that society and that small but honoured band of enlightened people who have contributed to what is most valuable and durable for Scotland in its policy, are entitled to our special recognition and gratitude.

The book also owes much to the stimulation of my friends in Scottish dance and music, without whose questions and enthusiasm the idea behind it may never have been inspired. My wife Catherine and our dancing children, Mark and Rosslyn, have contributed in all sorts of ways that I am happy to acknowledge. Nor can I forget the crucial practical help of Charles Grant with the illustrations and of Marian Burke and Elizabeth Milliken with the typing of the text, all have earned my sincerest gratitude.

George S. Emmerson

London, Ontario
1980

THE SCOTTISH COUNTRY DANCE

The term 'Country Dance' has now a very special meaning for dancers, it is the name of a particular form of social dance involving several couples in a series of figures which vary from dance to dance and is principally characterized by its longwise formation and its system of progression of each 'dancing couple' in turn. This dance form was a peculiarly English mutation of the native social dance forms of the British Isles. Not every folk dance of the countryside is therefore embraced by this special use of the term 'Country Dance'. The distinction arose in England in the following way:

In medieval times, the social folk dances of the British Isles were variously classified as *heys, hornpipes, rounds, jigs* and *reels*, and they varied in character, as did their music, from region to region. The ritualistic dances — the Morris dances and the sword dances — belong to a separate category. At Court, however, where more cultivated fashions prevailed, the more formal products of the celebrated dancing masters of Florence and France were assiduously practiced and performed to correspondingly formal music which was nevertheless often framed upon folk dance rhythms. Such, indeed, were the beginnings of ballet and the developing art of European music.

No English courts were more partial to the formal arts of music and dance than were those of the Tudors and particularly the Court of Elizabeth. Alongside this developed an increasing national consciousness and sense of dominion which placed new pride in all that was of England and of her yeomen. The social dances of the English countryside and their much loved and characteristic tunes, therefore, found increasing acceptance at Elizabeth's Court and soon it was the regular practice to close an evening of formal dances with one or two of the native country dances in which the servants participated. So popular did this become in Court circles after Elizabeth's reign that the dancing masters introduced some of their own devising, in which it appears that they were probably influenced by the similar strain of figured dances *(Contrapassi)* referred to in the books of the Italian dancing masters Caroso and Negri, with which they were familiar. Some of these dances were first exhibited in the Court masques which were a favourite diversion of the period, usually in simulated rural settings.

In such a way, then, did the English Country Dance acquire its special name and identity. These dances were in the form of square, round and longwise formations. But it was not until about fifty years after Elizabeth that the first collection of these appeared in print. This occurred in a curious way.

The lawyers in training at the Inns of Court in London were very partial to 'country dancing' at their festivities and thus it arose that John Playford, their bookseller, published a collection of them in 1651, the year in which the Civil War ended, and, more startlingly, in which Cromwell's puritanical rule began. This work was destined to run to about seventeen editions in the next seventy years. The tunes to which the dances were set and which gave them their names were mostly traditional song tunes, many of them Scottish and Irish.

At this time there was no Court to form a focal point of society in Edinburgh as in London, and, in any case, the temper of Scotland in the seventeenth century was not conducive to the indulgence of formal dance assemblies, although people of all ranks certainly danced on social occasions.

The dances of the countryside of Scotland and Ireland were referred to as 'reels', 'jigs' and 'hornpipes' by all classes; there was no occasion for townspeople to refer to them as 'country' dances. In at least one important instance in the sixteenth century we find them, in Scotland, being called 'licht' dances — obviously to distinguish them from the 'grave' dances of the Court. Certain Irish dances, such as *Trenchmore* and *The Irish Hey*, were much in

2

vogue in Elizabethan England, and there is every reason to believe that some of the English country dances were common to lowland Scotland and the North of England.

By the close of the seventeenth century, the formal Country Dance had attained a considerable vogue in English society. Almost all the favourite dances were then of the longwise variety suitable for the long galleries of the great houses, and incorporating the ingenious artifice of 'progression' of each 'dancing couple' in turn. This was the style of 'Country Dance' then exported to France and thence to other European centres, and even also to Edinburgh, and to which the term 'Country Dance' thenceforth uniquely applied.

Early in the eighteenth century, the ancient Kingdom of the Scots, now sharing its monarch with England, Ireland and Wales, entered into an incorporating union with the auld enemy. After a decade or two of uneasy development and one last constitutional convulsion, as we may call the Jacobite Rebellion of 1745-6, the Scottish genius settled down to expressing itself to the world, and establishing new communities, nay, new nations, and giving the improved steam engine, among other things, philosophical, technological, medical and scientific, to mankind. Edinburgh quickly became an intellectual centre of considerable force, taking its place in the hierarchy of European capitals in no uncertain way; its literati contributing to the enlightenment which began to relieve the shadows on men's minds in Europe. Some of the characteristics of cultivated life in Paris and London were now emulated amidst the wynds and lands of the 'Athens of the North'. Balls and assemblies in Auld Reekie largely followed the pattern of their counterparts in London and Bath and other English centres of fashion, and were soon to be followed by like institutions in Glasgow, Aberdeen, Leith, Haddington, Perth and Inverness, wherever some kind of social élite could concentrate.

The dance assemblies were conducted with the greatest decorum, and each evening of dancing invariably began with Minuets and concluded with Country Dances. The prevailing longwise formation, and the conviction, for which there was every justification, that all *formal* social dances were French, led many in ensuing years to regard the word 'country' as a corruption of the French *contre*, and this idea gained wide currency in the nineteenth century. Indeed, in North America especially, Country Dances were called *contradances*. The French, however, did develop a similar dance form in the eighteenth century which they called *Contredanse* or *Cotillon*. From this was derived the *Quadrille*, which largely superseded the Country Dance in formal nine-

Farmed Lands 1747-55, Mainland of Scotland

Enclosed farmed land is shown in black and unenclosed stippled. The most striking feature is the limited extent of cropped land, especially in the Northeast, together with the minor proportion which is enclosed.

Source: Roy's Map of Scotland, 1747-55
(British Museum MS. K.XLVIII. 25. 8,
Table and Maps 175 + 3).

4

teenth century assemblies in England and which returned the debt to the countryside by developing as a rural dance in North America, the 'square dance', so named after its formation.

As has been mentioned, many of the Country Dances published in England, in the seventeenth century and later, were set to Scottish tunes and consequently bore Scottish titles, the dances being named after their tunes. This, of course, did not make them Scottish dances; but some of them probably were. The technique was rudimentary and arbitrary, although certain steps were taught by English dancing masters for Country Dancing in the eighteenth century including what were called 'Scotch' steps.

Meantime, the Scots proceeded to absorb the English longwise progressive Country Dance as a fashionable dance form recognizably related to their own tradition of dance and music.

Precisely how it took root in Scotland is not easy to determine; but one important and obvious way was through the select dance assemblies and private balls of the growing towns of the Lowlands. We trace them in the Scottish countryside, too, by the middle of the eighteenth century, in certain regions of the East coast, and in the South-West and Border country. The itinerant dancing master taught a range of Country Dances in his circuit; all of which coincided with the aspiring spirit of eighteenth century Scottish life. Nowhere, we are told by an Englishman, Captain Topham, was dancing regarded as so essential a part of polite education as in Edinburgh. (*Letters from Edinburgh*, 1775.)

The indigenous dances of Scotland were of the same strain as those of Ireland and England. But among the Scottish Highlanders there was a tradition of dancing of a unique sophistication of technique and grace of style which seems to have especially flowered in the glens among the Grampian mountains, particularly in the broad valley of the River Spey (Strathspey). The favourite social dance of these regions, the *Highland Reel*, was a dance for three or four people who alternately 'reeled' and 'set'. The steps were precise and varied, and are familiar to all who have seen dancers at Highland games.

This dance, called *The Scotch Reel* in England and Europe generally, was executed to the vigorous native dance tunes in quadruple time and also to a style of these which was identified with Strathspey and took that name. The combination of the two, 32 bars of Strathspey followed by the same of 'Reel' was very popular in the nineteenth century and called simply *Strathspey and Reel* or *Foursome Reel*. Another reel belonging to the same tradition was *The Reel o' Tulloch*, one of the crowning glories of Scottish traditional social dance, which is discussed later in this

5

book, as is the popular *Eightsome Reel* which evolved as a combination of *Quadrille* and *Highland Reel* in the later nineteenth century. The *Highland Reel* and its relatives are not Country Dances, by definition, although they are dances of the Scottish countryside. Nevertheless, the Royal Scottish Country Dance Society has very rightly included these dances in its collection, for they involve all that is most peculiar, characteristic and distinguished in Scotland's contribution to the social dance of Europe. (To be really precise, the R.S.C.D.S. should perhaps have been named the 'Royal Scottish Traditional Social Dance Society'.)

Here we have love of dancing *per se*, vigorous elaboration of step and energetic movement. If there is grace, it is the grace of the *Strathspey*, a sprightly filagree of control of foot and limb and elevation; not the restrained risings and fallings of the *Minuet* — to which Scots, and Irish too, were somewhat alien in temperament — but the grace of agile movement harking back to the *Galliard* of the sixteenth century.

Certainly, the popular taste was boisterous at many a romp in barn or on the green, and the picture of the dance in Alloway's 'auld haunted kirk' seems altogether characteristic of Scottish taste at its most rudimentary:

> The piper loud and louder blew
> The dancers quick and quicker flew
> They reel'd, they set, they cross'd, they cleekit,
> Till ilka carlin swat and reekit,
> And coost her duddies tae the wark,
> And linkit at it in her sark!

The Scot had to move in the dance, and, at its best, with the grace of the deer rather than of the swan. Visitors to Atholl and Strathspey have left ample testimony to the delightful dancing they saw there in the eighteenth century; just as others deplored what they thought a lack of grace or poise in the dancing of the Lowland assemblies. There are numerous indications, however, that the Scots shared the French reverence for the cultivated art of dance as a worthy end in itself.

Yates, an English dancing master of a celebrated dancing family, wrote as follows about *The Scotch Reel* in 1822: (G. Yates: *The Ball; or A Glance at Almack's*, London, 1822.)

> When well danced, it has a very pleasing effect; nothing can be imagined more lively and brilliant than the steps in many of the Scotch dances, and the natives show as much enthusiasm for their own style of dancing as the French feel, if not more; for the Scotch are ready to dance a reel, morning, noon, or night, and they never seem to know when to leave off.

Nearly forty years later, a Boston dancing master writes of the same dance in a similar vein:

> The Scots are indefatigable in this dance, and while engaging in it, seem to become almost intoxicated. They snap their fingers, throw their arms and legs about in a wild manner, cry aloud, and perform difficult steps so quickly that the eye can scarce follow them.
> The figure is danced by two ladies and two gentlemen, forming a line of four, the ladies in the centre. They begin with a chain in passing between each other, until the gentlemen return to their places. The ladies finish by facing the gentlemen; then they balance before each other, the gentlemen exerting their utmost skill, while the ladies dance quietly. After eight bars, they begin again and chain and set, and this they continue to do as long as strength permits, yet seeming never to grow weary, but rather to acquire new vigour at each balance.

This then, was how the world saw Scottish dancing. Yet there were many other reels, some slightly modified forms of the same reel, particularly in the West Highlands, Orkney and Shetland, Sutherland, Buchan, the Mearns and Perthshire. Some of these were for six or eight dancers in 'longwise' formation, but without the progression device which distinguished the Country Dance, and nearly all exploited the reel figure almost exclusively, whereas many Country Dances were constructed of other figures with names like 'right and left', 'down the middle', 'cast off', 'whole figure' and so on.

As the eighteenth century progressed, more and more Country Dances were devised to Scottish dance tunes — Strathspeys, Reels, Rants, Scottish Measures, Hornpipes, Jigs and Marches — and these were compiled in London publications for sale in England as well as Scotland. Enthusiastic amateurs and dancing masters compiled collections of their own, some of which survive in manuscript. The figure: set-to-and-turn-corners-and-reel-on-the-sides, was introduced; obviously derived from *The Highland Reel*. The Scots brought to the longwise progressive Country Dance their music and step tradition and their feeling for movement and made it their own.

The Country Dance died out in England in the early nineteenth century, in a flurry of chaos and indifference, while maturing in a healthier mutation in the Scottish countryside. Many Country Dances were now staple fare alongside the ubiquitous *Haymakers* (also known as *Sir Roger de Coverley* in England, and *Virginia Reel* in North America), *The Scotch Reel, Babbity Bowster* and the *Bumpkin*. The Borders and East Coast Lowlands were its strongest habitats, and it persisted there at kirn, bridal and fair, although increasingly succumbing to the new couples dances, and in the more formal balls of the towns, to the *Quadrille*, particularly in its form of the *Lancers*. *The Highland Schottisch*, or *Scottish Polka*, introduced in the later decades of the nineteenth century, drew its substance from the Scottish tradition; but few of these dances, let alone the Scottish Country Dance, survived the First World War.

For a few years after that destructive and epoch-shaking war, it was possible to encounter such dances as *The Foursome Reel, Reel o' Tulloch, Eightsome Reel, Strip-the-Willow, Petronella, Circassian Circle, Dashing White Sergeant, Triumph, Rory O' More, Haymakers* and *Flowers of Edinburgh* at such balls as the Perth Hunt and Glasgow Police, and at weddings and like domestic occasions — at which older people felt free to participate with the young. But the traditional fiddlers seemed a dying species, and the melodeon or accordion, with the so-called bothy bands, became increasingly popular for country hops.

There was some loss of grasp of the traditional style in both music and social dance. The Industrial Revolution and the depopulation of the Highlands had taken their toll, as well as had the new fashions in dancing. Now, when *The Scotch Reel* or *The Eightsome Reel* were danced, it was as a rowdy travesty. *Strip-the-Willow* became nothing more than a violent scramble. Here indeed was a nation's degradation. It was the age of cosmopolitan Jazz and Swing and their derivatives and no one would have predicted

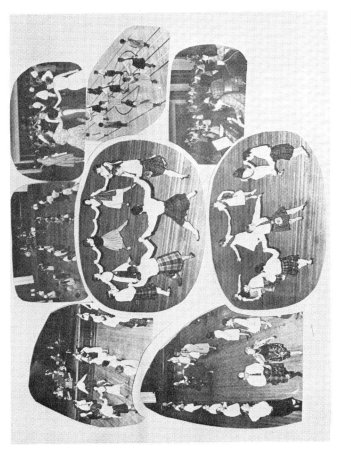

DANCERS AT A "SEMI-FORMAL" SCOTTISH COUNTRY DANCE

(with acknowledgments to the Bog-Cotton Circle, U.W.O., Ontario)

1. Crossing to own side
4. "Lead down the middle"

2. Longwise sets assembling
5. "Eight hands round" (Strathspey)
7. Chain figure (Strathspey)

3. "Four Hands Across"
6. "Down the middle and up" (Strathspey)
8. Band with dancers "unwinding"
   from *Allemande* in background

9

that the traditional dance music, songs and dances, were due to enter a renaissance. To the demise of Scotland's traditional social dances and their music, there was no possible alternative in sight.

This period, however, saw also a groping for a restoration of the cultural identity of Scotland. It manifested itself in many ways, some obvious and some obscure. Hugh MacDiarmid turned to the languages and literature of Scotland and startled Scots by his use of the old language for poetry of universal theme and high intellectual import. Here was a dramatic breakaway from the 'parish pump' associations which had stifled Scottish poetry in the Lowland tongue since Burns. The repercussions on all walks of Scottish cultural life were incalculable.

On another plane, a symptom of the same impulse, Mrs. Stewart of Fasnacloich, bearer of a name distinguished in the Gaelic lore of Appin and Argyll generally, was seized of the idea of restoring and re-introducing the old social dances of Scotland, and of course, with them, their music. She found a person rather uniquely fitted to further her grand intention, in Miss Jean C. Milligan, at that time in charge of Physical Education instruction at the Jordanhill Teacher's Training College, Glasgow, and together, in 1923, they founded what was to become the Royal Scottish Country Dance Society. The present book is a testimonial to the abundant fruit of that high endeavour.

The Scottish Country Dance, like a rare species facing extinction, has had to be protected and cultivated in its alien environment with much care and passion. Now it counts thousands of devotees throughout the world who meet together at classes, balls and dances, uplifted and inspired by the music and its associations with an ancestry which gave Scotland form and renown.

[For a more detailed discussion of this subject, see the author's *A Social History of Scottish Dance* (McGill-Queens) 1969.]

SCOTTISH COUNTRY DANCE MUSIC

Niel Gow

Scottish traditional dance music comprises several classes of dance rhythm which fall under the general heads of *reel*, *jig* and *hornpipe*. In the category of *reel* are embraced *rants*, *Scottish measures* and *Strathspeys* — the common-time dance measures which, of old, formed the favourite dance music of the Scots. The category of *jig* embraces three or four distinctive triplet rhythms in 6/8 time; that of *hornpipe* the common-time derivative of the Scottish Measure (e.g. *College Hornpipe*) which dates from the eighteenth century as well as the older, original rhythm in 3/2 or 6/4 (e.g. *The Dusty Miller*). Country Dances have been set to tunes belonging to all these categories, but those to 3/2 hornpipes (employing Minuet steps) dropped out of countenance in the late eighteenth century and have never enjoyed favour in Scottish rural assemblies at any time. Nevertheless at least two dances to tunes in triple time — although not hornpipe rhythm — are included in the collection of the R.S.C.D.S. — *The Yellow Haired Laddie* and *Tweedside*, two well known Scottish songs of former times and neglected oddities in the Country Dance repertoire.

A few Scottish Country Dances are set to jigs and 4/4 and 2/4 marches which are neither traditional nor particularly Scottish, and in recent years there has been the introduction of Country Dances set to slow airs, even cradle songs (e.g. Skinner's *Forres Cradle Song*) and, one might say 'mockingly', called Strathspeys. These are not to be confused with the expressive 'slow' Strathspey of the Country Dance which inspires an expressive dance technique, rather are they 'walk-throughs' to music to which one feels more inspired to sing - or meditate - than dance.

Fortunately we have not yet been set the question, but if the trend continues it shall arise - what is to be said of a 'Strathspey' Country Dance set to *The Lost Chord* or, in a more sprightly vein for that matter, *Waltzing Matilda*? Is there a line to be drawn as far as *Scottish* Country Dance is concerned? No such questions can arise with the original Highland Strathspey. The answer shall be influenced by our conception of the tradition and of the meaning of the word 'Scottish' with respect to Country Dance.

The *Irish Hornpipe* is used sometimes in Scottish Country Dancing in mistake for the *Strathspey* which it resembles and, of course, Ireland is the fountainhead of the jig. Irish rants, too, are in great abundance and are irresistibly lively and exciting. As one would expect there have been extensive mutual borrowings and adoptions between the musicians of both countries, and Scottish Country Dancing would be much the poorer if it lost its Irish jigs and rants. There is less of English traditional music descernible in the repertoire except for a jig here and there.

The cultural affinities of the peoples of the British Isles are not surprising. The wonder is that within such a small area so great a musical diversity can be found. Many tunes are borrowed and shared between the regions and all that distinguishes their national character in many instances is little more than their rhythmical shape in performance. In one form the tune assumes an Irish identity, in another, Scottish.

Traditional music emerges in a mysterious way from the people, much in the way a joke emerges and travels from place to place taking on embroideries and variations of the original idea according to the teller but remaining identifiably the same joke. In this way, one could say that a 'joke' was a product of the people, but, at the same time, it had an originator, a creator.

In the case of a tune, the musician is influenced by the melodic and tonal clichés, as we might call them, on which he was raised. He is also very greatly influenced by his instrument, and of course so also are the melodic and tonal clichés. The voice is seldom of its own an innovator, rather is it an imitator; but in imitating, it is influenced by language and this in turn influences the rhythmic caste of its music. So arises, one supposes, a national music. When tunes could be written down and published, they could be claimed for their composer, and they could be frozen, as it were, in their original form. Left to oral transmission, variations are introduced by each performer. The published tunes of the great eighteenth century fiddlers have been identified with them in a way that was impossible for the fiddlers or pipers of previous times; a new era in the transmission of traditional tunes had dawned. In addition, there was much prestige for the good fiddler. He was much in demand at country mansions as well as rural barns, and dancing had not been so popular in all walks of life for over a century.

Niel Gow's celebrity owes as much to his good fortune of being born in the eighteenth century as from his undoubted genius in the native musical idoms. His sons, William, John and Nathaniel, followed in his footsteps, and many a great dancing occasion was not arranged until Niel Gow's presence was assured. His son Nathaniel enjoyed a similar prestige, and created what must have been the first itinerant Scottish dance band. Neil Gow usually performed alone, with his brother Donald on the 'cello, the fiddler and his bass being the favourite combination for Scottish dance music in their day. The bagpipe was favourite out of doors, although it must be remembered that there were at least four distinct styles of bagpipe to be found in earlier times in the Scottish countryside.

The Great Pipe of the Highlands was an instrument of state for which use on 'small' music, as dance music was called, was regarded by the true Highlander as an indignity. An exact replica of the Great Pipe to a smaller scale, sometimes called a 'Reel-Set', was, however, used for dancing in the Highlands. The Jews' harp was also much used, as well as 'Mouth-Music' (*Port-a-Beul*).

Nowadays, the accordion has usurped the place of the fiddle in playing for dancers, largely on account of its greater volume of sound and its utility in filling in harmony. Electronic amplifiers have also come into use. Keyboard instruments, however, are limited in the matter of tonality and, of course, certain runs and leaps which are possible on the fiddle are not easy on a keyboard. These are limitations which may have a considerable effect on Scottish traditional dance music, and Irish too, in the future.

There is a growing community of Scottish fiddlers but they do not usually seek employment as accompanists to dancing in the old way. Their tradition too lives on, and indeed is thriving in Canada and other regions which owe much of their culture to Scottish settlement.

13

Tunes in the traditional idom are still being composed, and are finding their way into print. Many of our favourite reels and Strathspeys, however, were composed by William Marshall, 'Red Rob' Mackintosh, Daniel Dow, Angus Cumming and Niel and Nathaniel Gow, to mention only the most celebrated. These take us from the late eighteenth century into the nineteenth and many fiddlers contributed to the repertoire throughout the nineteenth centure. Of these, the distinguished J. Scott-Skinner bridged the gap into the twentieth century.

Skinner was a trained violinist. Few of the older fiddlers emulated the violinist's bowing action, nor indeed did they hold up their instrument as the trained violinist does. Skinner also introduced a degree of chromaticism into some of his tunes which is not found in the traditional strain; but the best of them are worthy of our high regard and have found a permanent place.

Country Dances are usually published with their principal tunes although only occasionally adhering to the old practice of taking the names of the tunes. It is surely an affront to traditional usage, however, to name a dance after a celebrated tune or song — such as *The Campbells are Coming*, or *Auld Lang Syne*, or *Seann Triubhas Willichan* — then set the dance to another tune entirely.

The repetition of the one tune throughout a particular dance would be unbearable today, however acceptable it may have been in former times. Consequently the intelligent musician supplements the 'name' or designated tune of each dance with others at his own discretion. The art of matching these in style and key and mood to each other and to the dance itself is what distinguishes the first rank of Scottish Country Dance musicians.

As regards tempo; this is intimately related to the technique of the dance, the skill of the dancers and the condition of the floor on which they dance. The inferior dancer prefers a faster tempo than the more accomplished. It is incumbent upon the musician to perceive the optimum tempo in the circumstances. Spacious tempi enable the dancer to articulate, but unless there is also bite, drive and nuance in the musical expression, the Scottish spirit, which is nothing if not vital, may be lost.

[For further information on this subject the reader should refer to the author's *Rantin' Pipe and Tremblin' String* (J.M. Dent, 1971).]

DRESS FOR SCOTTISH COUNTRY DANCING

There are no hard and fast rules regarding dress for Scottish Country Dancing. It is nowadays usual and comfortable for the men to wear the kilt with shirt and tie and the ladies, a dress or skirt and blouse. On formal occasions, especially, the ladies wear a tartan sash and often a white dress is preferred; the men wear Highland evening dress. Soft dancing slippers are appropriate.

The Ladies' Sash

There is probably no more controversial issue in dress for Scottish Country Dancing than how the ladies sash should be worn. Miss Milligan of the R.S.C.D.S. claimed that the sash is a remnant of the plaid or shawl so widely used as a general sort of over-garment or cloak by the women of Highland and Lowland Scotland right into recent times, and which was used by the mother to support and cover her baby, which she held in her left arm, thus leaving the right arm free. It follows, that she wore the plaid for this purpose over her left shoulder.

Sir Thomas Innes of Learney, the Lord Lyon King-of-Arms, however, approves three styles of wearing the sash as follows:

(1) *Style worn by Clanswomen*
The sash is worn over the right shoulder across the breast to the waist, across the back over the right shoulder and is secured by a pin or small brooch on the right shoulder.

(2) *Style worn by Wives of Clan Chiefs and Wives of Colonels of Scottish Regiments*
The sash, which may be rather fuller (24 in. wide with 12 in. fringe) is worn over the left shoulder across the breast to the waist across the back over the left shoulder and secured with a brooch on the left shoulder.

(3) *Style worn by Ladies who have married out of their Clan*
but who wish to use their original clan tartan. The sash, usually longer than style (1), is worn over the right shoulder, secured there with a pin and fastened in a large bow on the left hip.

It follows that ladies who do not conform to any of the above categories are not left with much choice, for the normal person has only two shoulders over which to drape the sash. Most Country Dancers to-day favour style (2), so that the right arm is given greater freedom. Other ways in which the sash may be worn in Country Dancing, are:

(4)   Approved by Lord Lyon for Country Dancing, or where any lady desires to keep the front of the dress clear of the sash (as for example when wearing the riband of a chivalric order or any orders and decorations). This style is similar to the belted plaid and is really a small arisaid(see p. 23). It is attached to the dress at the back of the waist, perhaps by a small belt, and at the right shoulder by a pin or brooch so that the ends fall backward from the right shoulder and hang behind the right arm.

(5)   A style which takes the sash away from the shoulder altogether and which can look very distinctive and becoming on a person who wishes to avoid a crowded appearance at the shoulders and rejects style (4) because she wishes to have some tartan to the front of her dress.

It is interesting to read what Susan Sibbald has to say about the wearing of the sash at a Caledonian Ball in London around 1805.

We ladies wore white dresses; the scarf, not very wide, was over the right shoulder, and tied with a loose knot under the left arm, fringed ends, one longer than the other; a sash, not long, round our waists, tied behind. (*Memoirs of Susan Sibbald*, London, 1926.)

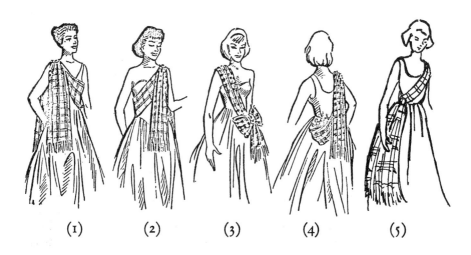

(1)   (2)   (3)   (4)   (5)

16

Male Highland Dress

The male Highland dress is much more elaborate. To-day there are certain distinctive styles of evening dress which have evolved from the ceremonial dress of Clan chiefs in the eighteenth century and earlier, and by way of the Highland regiments. Common to all are the dress tartan kilt, dress sporran, kilt pin and fully diced hose. The variations lie in the jacket and tie, the basic styles of which are:

(1) *Montrose Doublet*
Velvet or cloth, black or of a colour to blend with the kilt, silver buttons of Celtic design, leather belt with silver buckle, lace jabot.

(2) *Sheriffmuir Coat*
Velvet or cloth, black or of a colour to blend with the kilt. Silver buttons, matching or tartan vest, white shirt with turn-down collar or stiff shirt with wing collar, black bow tie or lace jabot.

Montrose doublet   Sherriffmuir coat   Prince Charlie Coatee   Regulation Doublet   Kenmore Doublet

17

(3) *Prince Charlie Coatee*
Black cloth with silk facings or velvet of a colour to blend with
the kilt; silver buttons, matching or tartan vest; white shirt with
turn-down collar or stiff shirt with wing collar; black bow tie or
lace jabot.

Lace ruffles at the cuffs may be worn when the jabot is worn.
A silver brooch mounted with cairngorms may be worn on the
jabot.
Skean Dhu is worn in the stocking on the right leg.
Green or red garters and flashes.
For dancing, black ghillie shoes should be worn.
Otherwise the shoes should be patent leather dress brogues with
strap and buckle or 'gillie' lacing.

It is a strange fact that non-Scots tend to wear the kilt too
long, and the hose too high ('choking the knees'). The kilt should
not extend below the knee-cap, nor droop excessively at the back.

(4) *Regulation Doublet*
Black cloth, peak or notch lapels, silk facings, silver buttons,
matching or tartan vest, shoulder straps, gauntlet cuffs and
Inverness flaps. Shirt as for Prince Charlie Coatee.

(5) *Kenmore Doublet*
Cloth or velvet, black or of a colour to blend with the kilt.
Single breasted with a stand collar and lace jabot.

Formal Male Dress for Country Dancing

Strictly formal dress has been described above and this is *de
rigeur* at strictly formal Scottish Country Dance occasions. There
is no doubt, however, that formal Highland dress was not devised
for Scottish dancing. The practical exigencies of this demand a less
confining garment, especially in those parts of the world where
room temperatures are, on the average, higher than they are in
Scotland.

For this reason, it has become more and more acceptable to
resort to white shirt and tie as the evening progresses. This, in itself, is acceptable informal dress with plain leather sporran and
hose. However, compromise is often called for in Scottish Country
Dancing and the satin or silk blouse-sleeved shirt with jabot and
lace cuffs, is an excellent one. In this case, dress sporran and diced
hose may be worn.

Of the styles considered here, only the Montrose and Kenmore doublets require a dress belt. The dress belt may also appropriately be worn with the blouse-sleeved shirt, as this is a

formal style in its own right. Strictly speaking, the dress belt is inappropriate with the informal dress, although a belt is often felt to be acceptable at Scottish Country Dance occasions of semi-formal pretentions, it gives a more finished appearance, and less the look of someone who has just doffed his jacket.

By the same token, to wear the waistcoat or vest without the jacket is indeed to have just that undressed appearance; and is therefore obviously wrong.

Informal Dress - Tweed Jacket:

An ordinary jacket is unacceptable with the kilt. The tweed jacket used with the kilt has a special cut and often has special cuffs and shoulder straps. The buttons are of leather or bone. The appropriate cap is the Balmoral Bonnet, and the shoes, brogues. Plain woollen hose, with or without flashes, and plain leather sporran and plain tie complete the informal ensemble.

THE KILT

These, then, are our guide-lines in the matter of dress. It seems altogether unnecessary to explain that the kilt is a male garment and therefore should never be worn by ladies. It has the additional disadvantage from a feminine point of view, of exaggerating the hips. From this has emerged the tartan skirt, often tailored after the fashion of a kilt but longer, and of lighter material.

I have more to say about the history of Highland dress in the sections, *Tartan Plaid* and *Tartan Trews.* Suffice it here to pass some remarks on the social circumstances and varying attitudes towards the kilt in the past two centuries or so.

The belted plaid gave way to the kilt as the eighteenth century progressed. The trews, as we shall see, were an ancient Celtic garment, and were associated with Highland gentlemen in that century. The burgesses of the Lowland burghs were wont to regard the Highlander as something of a savage and his dress accordingly suffered from this association.

In the early years of the nineteenth century, Dalyell, the Scottish music historian, visited the Trossachs along with the Laird of Macnab — undoubtedly the same whose dark and stormy aspect has been set so unforgettably against a dark and stormy sky by the painter Raeburn — and when they passed Stirling Bridge to the eastward, he laid his kilt aside, holding such a costume not sufficiently decorous for the Lowlands.

As the same writer tells us: 'No reputable gentleman would have appeared in a kilt in the streets of Edinburgh; and I recollect some expressions denoting surprise, not unmixed with disapprobation, from ladies, that a young Highlander, though a person of family of distinction, should appear in one at an evening party where I was present'.

The Highland regiments raised for the British Army in the eighteenth century wore the kilt and some of the officers must have attended London balls in this dress in the early nineteenth century if we can judge from Cruikshank's cartoon of 'The Fair Assembly'. Highland pipers, too, wore the kilt when they visited the Lowlands.

As numerous engravings show, the kilt was common wear among the Highland peasantry in the early nineteenth century, yet to-day it is rarely to be seen among them. It has, instead, become a garment of formal as opposed to working occasions, and has acquired an association with the laird which has earned it a kind of mark of social caste which it is felt presumptuous to emulate.

From being prohibited after the '45 and from the displacement of the bulk of the population and the disruption of the home weavers, the kilt lost ground. It now became more expensive than trews, for even in a modern kilt there are about eight to nine yards of tartan.

The appearance of King George IV in a kilt on his celebrated visit to Edinburgh in 1820 represented something of a breakthrough for the dress — and we owe much to Sir Walter Scott for this event. Twenty years or so later, Queen Victoria dressed her husband and family in the kilt, and even the Grand Duke Frederick of Germany, when he visited Balmoral was set up in all its finery. This undoubtedly gave Highland dress its supreme endorsement.

Even in the Lowlands, the kilt was very popular with young boys as the century progressed, and still is for informal as well as formal dress. Boy scouts, youth hostellers, mountaineers and others of the great outdoors have rediscovered the utility and comfort of the ancient garment while the Highlander follows his plough or his laird's guns, in trousers!

A considerable number of professional and businessmen now wear the kilt as everyday dress, and such is the power of association that they would certainly be unrecognized by their friends if they were seen in trousers.

The Industrial Revolution, the clearance of the Highlands and the revelation of the essential cultural unity of Scotland and the richness of its Celtic heritage have produced a new situation in which the kilt finds an honourable place. It is also without peer as the garment for the performance of Scottish dance, and like all tokens, great or small, which give identity to the ancient Kingdom, it is fondly cherished by the Scot himself as a symbol.

THE TARTAN PLAID

The plaid was the essential part of the dress of the Scottish Highlanders, serving as kilt and cloak and blanket. The cloths used for this were woven in variously coloured checks or stripes and called 'tartan'. The Highlander, then, wore a 'tartan' plaid. Material of this kind was sometimes called 'plaiden', or to anglify the word, 'plaiding'. The 'plaid', however, is the garment, 'tartan' is the cloth woven in the characteristic chequered patterns.

The association of particular patterns (setts) of tartan with particular family names or clans has its origin in the preferences of the people of particular regions and of family weavers for their own patterns. As Martin explains in the early eighteenth century, 'Every isle differs from each other in their fancy of making Plads as to the stripes in breadth and colours. The humour is as different through the mainland of the Highlands, in so far that they who have seen those places are able at the first view of a man's Plad, to guess the place of his residence.'

Martin goes on to say, 'When they travel on foot the Plad is tied on the breast with a bodkin of bone or wood . . . the Plad is tied round the middle with a leather belt; it is pleated from the belt to the knee very nicely'.

This form of plaid was called *feileadh-beag* ('philibeg'), literally, 'short cover' and sometimes 'kilt'. The wearer had to make the pleats himself each time he donned the garment. As long as the kilted plaid or *feileadh-beag* could be required as a blanket or wrap, it was not practical to make permanent pleats. However, it appears that, in the seventeenth century, fixed pleats were not unknown. The middle part of the plaid was formed into fixed pleats and about a yard either side was unpleated. The whole was then wrapped round the waist and the ends crossed over in front. This is the obvious progenitor of the kilt we know to-day.

However, the *breacan-feile* ('tartan covering') or 'belted plaid' is probably older. This garment is now in desuetude and, except in so far as the shoulder plaid reminds us of it, has not even ceremonial use to-day.

At one time, this could serve as the full clothing of the Highlander. It was wrapped round his body as decoratively as possible. A common way seems to have been to fasten the plaid round the waist with a belt to form a kilt and draw the remainder up behind to be fastened to the shoulder by a brooch or perhaps over the shoulder to a pin or brooch on the chest; the loose length being allowed to hang down behind. The plaid was pleated and folded to show off the sett of the tartan to best advantage. Much depended on the ornamental intention or purpose of the wearer of course.

The shoulder plaid of to-day is worn chiefly as an ornament, although such plaids were familiar among shepherds and trews-wearing Highlanders in earlier times.

When hose was worn with the belted plaid, it was 'half' hose — i.e., not above the knee, and usually only half-way up the calf of the leg. Shoes, when worn, were of raw cowhide and called quarrants or brogues.

The plaid was usually of about two yards in breadth and four in length. It was especially serviceable to the hunter or warrior, or even herdsman, in that land of mountain and flood. Lord President Forbes of Culloden, to whose manipulations the Hanoverian dynasty owed its survival, expressed the matter thus in a letter to the Lord Lyon of Scotland on the passing by the British Parliament of the act to prohibit the traditional Highland dress in 1746:

> The garb certainly fits men inured to it, to go through great fatigues, to make very quick marches, to bear out against the inclemency of the weather, to wade through rivers and shelter in huts, woods and rocks, upon occasions which men dressed in the lowland garb could not possibly endure. As the Highlanders are circumstanced at present it is, at least it seems to me, to be an utter impossibility without the advantage of this dress for the inhabitants to tend their cattle and go through the other parts of their business without which they could not subsist, not to speak of paying rents to their landlords.

The Act for the 'Abolition and Proscription of the Highland Dress' was only a part of the policy of extermination and genicide initiated by the failure of the Jacobite uprising in 1745. Its effective life was about twenty to thirty years, and it was repealed

(1782) primarily through the efforts of the Highland Society of London.

In speaking of Highland dress, a word about female attire may be appropriate.

The principal ancient garment was called the Arisaid; it was a plaid of light tartan, invariably on a white ground. The so-called 'dress Stewart', for instance, is an arisaid sett of the Stewart tartan. According to Martin, our informant quoted above, the arisaid reached from the neck to the heels and was tied in front, presumably by the two upper ends, and clasped to the breast by a 'buckle' of silver or brass according to the quality of the wearer. It was pleated all round and tied with a belt below the breast. 'They wore sleeves of scarlet cloth, closed at the end as men's vests, with gold lace round them, having plate buttons set with fine stones. The head dress was a fine kerchief of linen straight about the head, hanging down the back taperwise. A large lock of hair hangs down their cheeks above their breast, the lower end tied with a knot of ribands.'

What Martin calls a buckle is probably what we would call a brooch. The large one at the breast was engraved with various animals, and within it a smaller brooch comprising a large central stone surrounded by somewhat finer, but smaller, stones. The belt was a linkage of silver and leather.

There were doubtless other adornments according to the taste of the individual and Highland women would surely show as much inventiveness in this regard as their counterparts elsewhere. A number of very fine dress designs, some based on the arisaid, were elaborated from current styles in the seventeenth and eighteenth centuries by Highland ladies. The Flora Macdonald portraits are often cited as illustrations of these.

In the Lowlands, a seventeenth century English traveller wrote that the upper classes emulated French, German and English fashions. What he called 'the inferior sort of citizens' wives and the women of the countryside, 'did wear cloaks made of coarse stuff, of two or three colours, in checker work, vulgarly called ploden'. The Lowland countrymen wore a coarse cloth, 'hodden' as it was called, of a grey colour, and the blue bonnet. It was not customary for these to wear a plaid, excepting shepherds who spent long periods on the hill. The plaid was then often also of hodden grey and not always tartan.

The most marked departure from the ancient manners of dress occurred during the period of proscription, but in the early part of the nineteenth century it was possible to write of the inhabitants of the Highlands of Perthshire, for instance, that they spoke 'the Erse language', though most of them now spoke English also and that their dress was 'the ancient garb of the country, the bonnet, short coat, philibeg, and tartan hose'. The same could not be said by the year 1900.

In closing, something should be said of the word 'plaidie'. This is just a diminutive of the word 'plaid'. The use of such diminutive forms of certain words has been a habit of speech to a very marked degree in the regions surrounding the North-East coast of Scotland. The words 'laddie' and 'lassie', of course, are very general, and others appropriately used in speaking with children — affectionate terms — 'wee manie', 'wee lambie', 'wee doggie' have had a habit of finding their way into the familiar speech of adults. For some obscure reason, a further diminutive is often employed in the North-East — 'lassokie', 'manikie', 'lambikie' — where the syllables lend themselves to it.

The subject of Highland dress, is very fully treated by Frank Adam and Innes of Learney in their well-known book, *The Clans, Septs, and Regiments of the Scottish Highlands*, and by John Telfer Dunbar, *The History of Highland Dress*, O. & B. 1962.

YOUR TARTAN

Consult the lists available from any of the manufacturers of tartan cloth and you will be surprised at the number of names claiming title to a tartan. The whole subject of Scottish names is somewhat complicated. There is the clan name proper, those bound to it by bonds of manrent, those members of it who adopted another style of the name to distinguish them (which may be derived from the occupation, or from a physical peculiarity of the founder; or from the locality of a group). Then some names have been unaccountably anglicized.

The derived families are called *septs* or *cadets* of the clan, and all therefore lay claim to the tartan of their parent clan or to one of their own, often shared by districts served by the same weavers or conforming to the same fashions. However, a great range of distinctive tartans have emerged since the eighteenth century, a few produced by the military to distinguish certain regiments, e.g., *Black Watch*.

24

Some tartans have been devised on other excuses, such as the eighteenth century *Jacobite* and *Caledonia* tartans; the *Balmoral* tartan designed by the Prince Consort and reserved for the use of the Royal family; the tartan of the Young Chevalier (Prince Charlie's tartan) and the Nova Scotia tartan approved by Lord Lyon a few years ago, and others. So there is no need to be without a tartan if you feel you must justify your title to it.

TARTAN TREWS

It is commonly assumed to-day that the peculiarly Celtic contribution to the sartorial fashions of Europe is the kilt. The truth of the matter, however, will seem incredible and paradoxical — the Roman dress was the toga, or mantle, and the belted tunic, closely resembling the plaid and kilt, at a time when the Celts were wearing breeches or trousers. The Celtic contribution, then, was really trousers! The Romans nicknamed the Celtic druids — as they were encountered in France — 'the long-trousered philosophers', and although there was much prejudice among the Romans against the trousers of the transalpine people, the Celtic garment triumphed in time.

A French authority (M. D'Arbois de Jubainville, *Les Celtes* (Paris, 1904).) points to the use of trousers by the Gauls as early as the third century B.C., at which time they also wore mantles, or plaids, for the upper part of the body. He asserts that the Gauls derived the lower garment from the Germans who had derived it from the Scythians and these in turn from the Iranians.

The reports of the Roman historians and other evidence clearly establish that the tartan, in varied colours, with red or crimson predominating, was fully established among the Celts of Britain two thousand years ago. The dress of the period being a sleeved blouse, often belted, with a tartan plaid thrown over it; the lower limbs being clad in trews, closely fitting at the ankle.

There are many, more recent, descriptions of the place of trews in Highland dress which can be quoted but we will restrict ourselves to just a few of these. An interesting entry in the Accounts of the Lord High Treasurer of Scotland describes the dress worn by James V during a hunting expedition in the Highlands in August 1538 — A 'short Highland coat' of parti-coloured velvet, lined with green taffety, '3 ells of Highland tartan to be hose', and a long and full 'Highland shirt' of holland cloth, with ribbons at the wrists. (The 'hose' here, is long hose. Stockings were called 'short hose').

Martin, writing of the Western Islanders in the reign of Queen Anne, tells us:

> Many of the people wear *trowis*, some of them very fine woven, like stockings of those made of cloth; some are coloured and others striped: the latter are as well shaped as the former, lying close to the body from the middle downwards, and tied round with a belt above the haunches. There is a square piece of cloth which hangs down before.

Other eighteenth century observers note that trews were worn by few except 'gentlemen', but Captain Burt, one of these observers, seems to give an explanation of this when he remarks that trews and plaid were 'chiefly their mode of dressing when they are in the Lowlands, or when they make a neighbouring visit, or go anywhere on horseback; but those among them who travel on foot, and have not attendants to carry them over the waters, vary it into the quelt'. The 'quelt' or kilt, very understandably then, for practical reasons was, in Burt's words, 'the common habit of the ordinary Highlanders'.

General Stewart of Garth tells us in 1822 that his grandfather 'always wore the Highland garb except when in mourning; that is, the truis on horseback, and the kilt when at home'.

There are many eighteenth century paintings showing Highland gentlemen in trews from which the elegant shape and style of the garment can be determined. Trousers of this style replaced breeches and hose in European dress as the nineteenth century advanced.

ETIQUETTE OF SCOTTISH COUNTRY DANCING

Etiquette, like fashion, varies with each generation and with circumstances. But while the forms vary, the underlying principles of consideration for the comfort, privacy, convenience, sensibilities and happiness of others, even at the expense of one's own, remain constant. Certainly there is an aspect of etiquette that is purely ceremonial or even ritualistic, which has its origin in the cultivated life of the aristocracy of past ages. The circumstances of life have changed and, central to it, as far as etiquette is concerned, so has the status of woman. Yet there is much grace and art in the courtesies of that former life and much that finds a natural surviv-al where the environment is conducive to it, as at a Scottish Coun-try Dance ball. But the rigid bands of what was called 'good-form' are released to make way for 'good-sense'. Etiquette now is a means to an end, not an end in itself.

The Scottish peasantry — and that of other countries too — had their own etiquette, although perhaps they never used that word. The visitor was always offered a dram when he called and a 'stirrup cup' ere he departed. The benighted wayfarer's name was never sought lest it should be that of a feuding family and thus come in the way of the hospitality which was his due. A cup of tea has taken the place of the dram in most families to-day, but it is used in the same way. The visitor arrives — the kettle goes on; he prepares to depart — it goes on again. It is a natural courtesy which one misses in other parts of the world.

The Scottish Country Dance ball presents some special prob-lems which distinguish it from others. It is usually a meeting of people interested in the dancing *per se*, and only incidentally a means to a social end. Something of the reverse pertains at a St. Andrew's Society or Caledonian Society ball, at which there usually is much Scottish Country Dancing; and even at some Roy-al Scottish Country Dance Society balls, though it is perhaps a little more difficult to justify this in a body devoted to the teach-ing of Country Dancing.

The following simple rules are generally observed everywhere:

1. Take your place in the sets at the end of the line as it is form-ed.
2. Do not form your set before the M.C. has announced the dance.
3. Do not dance with the one partner all evening, even if you are married to that partner.
4. Men, escort your partner to her seat on the completion of the dance.
5. Having taken a place in a set, you should never desert it un-til the dance is finished.

Each Country Dance, of course, begins and ends with a bow and curtsy.

27

Ladies, married or otherwise, are no longer offending society when they attend a Country Dance ball unescorted. In the absence of a male partner, ladies often dance together. It is still largely the man's privilege to ask the lady to dance, but at Scottish Country Dance occasions there is considerable commonsense easement of this among familiars.

The old difficulty of the lady's declining an invitation to dance then changing her mind when asked by another gentleman, still remains. My advice to men who are thus rejected is the same as that offered by writers on the subject a century ago — *seem not to notice it, for in these matters ladies are exempt from all explanations.* After all, the lady, denied the privilege of partner selection enjoyed by the male, is entitled to some licence in the matter. The lady's happiness surely comes before the preservation of male pride.

Ballroom and party etiquette was once a very voluminous subject. The Scottish Country Dance occasion retains as much of the old-world courtesy as seems still appropriate in our time and shares some of the general easing of formality to-day.

* * * * * *

Here are some extracts from ballroom manuals of a century ago which may amuse the reader:

From a New York publication 1864:

'Loud conversation, profanity, stamping the feet, writing on the wall, smoking tobacco, spitting or throwing anything on the floor, are strictly forbidden.'

'The practice of chewing tobacco and spitting on the floor, is not only nauseous to ladies, but is injurious to their dresses.'

'A gentleman should not address a lady unless he has been properly introduced.'

'No persons engaged in a dance that requires their assistance to complete the set should leave the room or sit down before the dance is finished.'

From a Boston publication 1858:

'Persons who have no ear for music, that is to say, a false one, ought to refrain from dancing.'

'Married or young ladies cannot leave a ballroom, or any other party alone. The former should be accompanied by one or two other married ladies, and the latter by their mother, or by a lady to represent her.'

'Ladies should avoid talking too much; it will occasion remarks. It has also a bad appearance to whisper continually in the ear of your partner.'

'In giving the hand for ladies' chain or any other figures, those dancing should wear a smile, and accompany it with a polite inclination of the head, in the manner of a salutation.'

'In public balls, a gentleman offers his partner refreshments, but which she very seldom accepts, unless she is well acquainted with him.'

From a Dundee publication 1890:

'Change partners often during the evening, in order that all may enjoy themselves. When requiring to use a handkerchief, put it in your pocket immediately when finished with it. Avoid all vulgar practices, such as biting your nails, making noise with the feet etc.'

And to go back over 150 years to *London* 1817:

'No person during a Country Dance, should hiss, clap, or make any other noise, to interrupt the good order of the company.'

'No Lady or Gentleman must, during a Country Dance, attempt at Reels, or any other Figures, in the same room.'

'Snapping the fingers, in Country Dancing and Reels, and the sudden howl or yell (introduced in some Scotch parties as partly national with them) ought particularly to be avoided, as partaking too much of the customs of barbarous nations.'

'No Dance ought to be performed twice the same evening.'

'Such persons as may dislike any Dance that is called, instead of interrupting the performance or endeavouring by any means to have the same altered, should retire to their seats.'

'Gentlemen are not allowed to enter the ballroom in boots, spurs, gaiters, trowsers, or with canes or sticks; nor are loose pantaloons considered proper for a Full Dress Ball.'

SCOTTISH COUNTRY DANCES

(from the R.S.C.D.S. Collection)

The Ale-Wife and her Barrel

This is the sad tale of the drunken Ale-wife who had the misfortune to have a taste for her product. Or rather, it is the lamentation of her suffering husband. A set of the tune is to be found in Christie's *Collection of Traditional Ballad Airs* (1876), and the set of verses given below are from Peter Buchan's MS. *Collection of the Songs of the North of Scotland*.

> My mind is vex'd and sair perplex'd,
> I'll tell you a' that grieves me;
> A drunken wife I ha'e at hame,
> Her noisome din aye deaves me.
> The ale-wife, the ale drunken wife,
> The ale-wife she grieves me;
> My wifie and her bar-re-lie
> They'll ruin me and deave me.
>
> She takes her barrel on her back,
> Her pint-stoup in her hand, O,
> And she is tae the market gane,
> For to set up a stand, O,
>   The ale-wife, &c.
>
> And when she does come hame again,
> She wades through girse and corn;
> Says, 'I maun hae anither pint,
> Though I should bed the morn'.
>   The ale-wife, &c.
>
> She sets her barrel on the ground,
> And travels but and ben, O;
> I canna get my wifie keepit
> Here awa' at hame, O.
>   The ale-wife, &c.

The dance is an exhilarating *tour de force* with much reaching of hands (reaching for the stoup!), changing of position and restless action as is appropriate to the theme.

Argyll (or Argyle) 'coastland of the Gael', has varied in extent since the name was first used. To-day the name embraces Kintyre, Knapdale and Cowal, and what is called Mid Argyll and North Argyll, the essential core of the old kingdom of Dalriada. The Scots, a prominent tribe established in Antrim, Northern Ireland, moved their central government there in the 5th century after considerable traffic between the two regions. In the year A.D. 498, the sons of Ere — Fergus, Loarn and Angus — took possession of certain localities: Fergus — Kintyre, Knapdale, Cowal and Mid Lorn; Loarn — lands in North Argyll; Angus — Islay. The principal tribes were named after Fergus' grandsons, Gabran and Comgall (Cowal), and after Loarn (Lorn) and Angus.

To-day, the territory of Argyll is associated with Clan Campbell, of which the chief is the Duke of Argyll. The territorial aggrandizement of this line began with the marriage of Gillespie Cambel to the heiress of the lands of the Lords of Lochow (Loch Awe), from whom descended Sir Colin Mor Campbell of Lochow, called Cailein Mor. From this is derived the patronymic of the successive chiefs of Clan Campbell. The second 'Lord Campbell' was created Earl of Argyll in 1457, beginning a line which continues to Archibald, Tenth Earl who was created Duke of Argyll in 1689.

The growth of the house of Argyll was largely made at the expense of MacDonald, Lord of the Isles, to whom James IV used Argyll as an effective counterpoise. The successive Earls became pillars of the state. Their power and apparent opportunism, led to their unpopularity with clans outside of the Campbell circle. The Seventh Earl perpetrated the brutal persecution of Clan Gregor which first blackened the Campbell name, and embarked on a similar commission against the MacDonalds. He was a tragically haunted man, and latterly fled to the Continent where he joined the Church of Rome. In contrast, his son, the First Marquis of Argyll (1641) led the Covenanting authority in Scotland in its dispute with King Charles I. The Marquis of Montrose, the 'Great Marquis', turned from the Covenanting forces to support the King when the Civil War broke out; preferring this to a theocracy ruled by Argyll. His subsequent triumphs have no place here, but he repeatedly humiliated Argyll in the field and invaded his territory with impunity.

There is deep irony in the ends of these great figures of the Scottish scene. Montrose was betrayed and captured while trying to raise an army to place Charles II on the throne and was executed for his pains. The Marquis of Argyll, not long after, was actually instrumental in bringing Charles II to Scotland, having him crowned and soon thereafter placed on the British throne. But such were the capricious ways of high-level politics and the violence of intolerance in these days that hardly a year had passed than Argyll himself was escorted down the Canongate to the Scaffold as Montrose had been before him, in expiation of his former activities against the royalists. His son also paid the supreme penalty (1685) for supporting Monmouth's rebellion. Such risks and sacrifices do not bespeak indifference. Whatever prejudices exist against Argyll, and they are widely perpetuated throughout the West Highlands to this day, several of the family have a deserving and undisputable claim to honour.

It was characteristic that the Second Duke, field-marshall and statesman, should be instrumental in introducing the Hanoverian dynasty, for although the House of Argyll owed much to the favour of the Stewart monarchs in earlier times, it provided a bulwark against the Jacobites in later times.

Argyll's Bowling Green seen from the head of Loch Long

George, the Eighth Duke, is distinguished for his scholarship. It is to him we owe the folk-lore activities of John Dewar, whose collection of Gaelic tales is only now beginning to be published. His son, best known as Lord Lorne, inherited some of these propensities, and became a Governor-General of Canada. Lorne's marriage to the Princess Louise, daughter of Queen Victoria, was a high point in the destiny of his family.

The antipathy between Clans Donald and Campbell is associated in people's minds with the infamous Massacre of Glencoe. But this shocking event was but an incident in a long-standing power conflict and, although perpetrated by Argyll's regiment of His Majesty's forces, was not instigated by Argyll as chief of the clan. On the other hand, Argyll's acquiescence is at least implied.

In all fairness, one must observe that treachery and barbarity justified by feud was an undeniable concomitant of the clan life of the Highlands. Although the Highlanders were civilized to a degree where that word connotes art and hospitality, there was a blight of violence in the temper, which perhaps, is not to be wondered at in a race of hunters living in a Northern clime of rock and torrent. When we think of it, however, we must conclude that the so-called Anglo-Saxon burghal community to the south — the 'Sassenachs' (southerners) — were no more virtuous, perhaps even less so, although perhaps more subtle and less violent.

The revolting aspect of the Glencoe incident was its deceitful and cynical exploitation of the basic rights of Highland hospitality. A company of Highlanders lived on the hospitality of fellow-Highlanders for twelve days, then put their hosts to the sword early in a snowy, bitter cold winter's morning, February 13, 1692. Herein lay the infamy.

Queen Victoria and Prince Albert visited Inveraray, the seat of Argyll, in 1847, during their celebrated tour of the West Highlands. Then in September 1875, by which time the Marquis was married to Princess Louise, the widowed Queen arrived at Inveraray by coach via Loch Awe. The beautiful house had received many famous visitors since it was rebuilt to the design of Roger Morris and Robert Mylne between 1747 and 1760. Boswell and Johnson called there in 1773 and followed the same road out of it, winding along the shores of Loch Fyne to the village of Cairn Dubh thence up the long and tortuous haul to the head of Glen Croe, than which rise Henry Cockburn thought few things more magnificent. It rained for Queen Victoria, unfortunately, and the trace horses refused their duty, but the sun broke through as her party descended into that magnificent, rock-strewn recess of deep blues, greens and purples. Up and over the craggy, serrated flank on her right were other frowning ranges and peaks, a rocky, mountainous morass which forms the gusset of Loch Goil and Loch Long. Ardgoil is its proper name, the 'promontory of the Gael', 'Argyll's Bowling Green' it has been facetiously called.

The name 'Argyll's Bowling Green' is not recent, for a tune of this title appears in early eighteenth century manuscripts, and a set of Country Dance figures is to be found attached to it in the

Holmain MS. Who devised the name or when it first arose is not known. The region was Gaelic-speaking until the nineteenth century, when General Wade developed the hill track through Glen Croe to Inveraray in 1748, his men set up a semicircular stone seat at the summit of the road bearing the injunction 'Rest and be Thankful'. This was despoiled by souvenir-hunters during the early nineteenth century. The road was gradually improved over the years although it retained its tortuous and irregular character. It has now been superseded by a modern carriageway which climbs the north flank of the Glen in a smooth, uniform gentle slope. The old road remains for all to see, twisting and turning like the burn alongside it, a memento of more romantic days, redolent of the illustrious people who have passed along it in wonder and admiration. Boswell and Johnson, Wordsworth, Burns, Pennant, Scott, Queen Victoria and so on, in the days before the automobile reduced the scale of the countryside. Apart from this, however, Argyll's Bowling Green is largely inaccessible to the motorist, but a paradise for the mountaineer and hillwalker within easy reach of Glasgow.

The mention of Queen Victoria at Inveraray in 1875, however, recalls her account of the dance given there to celebrate the occasion:

> At a quarter past ten we drove across to the temporary pavilion, where the ball to the tenants was to take place. Louise, Beatrice and Jane Churchill went with me in the Duke's coach. The Duke, Lorne and Colin received us, and the Duchess and all the girls and the other ladies were inside at the upper end on a raised platform, where we all sat. It is a very long and handsome room, I believe a hundred and thirty feet long, and was built at the time of Louise's marriage. It was handsomely decorated with flags, and there were present between seven and eight hundred people — tenants with their wives and families and many people from the town; but it was not like the Highland balls I have been accustomed to, as there were many other dances besides reels. The band could not play reels (which were played by the piper —, and yet came from Glasgow!) The ball began, however, with a reel; then came a Country dance, then another reel. Louise danced a reel with Brown, and Beatrice with one of the Duke's foresters; but the band could only play a Country dance tune for it. Another reel with pipes, in which Jane Churchill danced with Brown, and Francie Clark with Annie (Mrs. Macdonald, my wardrobe maid), Louise and Beatrice dancing in another reel with one of the other people and Mr. John Campbell. Then came a 'schottische', which seemed to be much liked there, and more reels, and lastly a 'tempete', in which Louise and Beatrice danced. In the early part a Gaelic song was sung by some of the people, including

Mr. John Campbell. I remember some which were sung by the boat-men on Loch Tay in 1842. After the 'tempete' we came away at nearly half-past twelve. *(Queen Victoria, More leaves from The Journal of a Life in the Highlands*, London, 1884 .)

The Axum Reel

This reel survived in North Ronaldshay into modern times and may, of course, be indigenous to that island. It is there a fav-ourite wedding dance, a class of 'bridal reel' of which several have been known in the Shetland and Hebridean islands. In Ronaldshay the bride and groom stood back to back with their arms linked while the Axum Reel was performed around them. After one or two times through the dance, the fiddler progressively changed from Strathspey to Reel and the dancers made about four com-plete circuits without setting. During this the fiddler stopped at his discretion and the bridal pair then rapidly tried to disentangle each other to kiss before the girls in the dance kissed the groom and the men the bride.

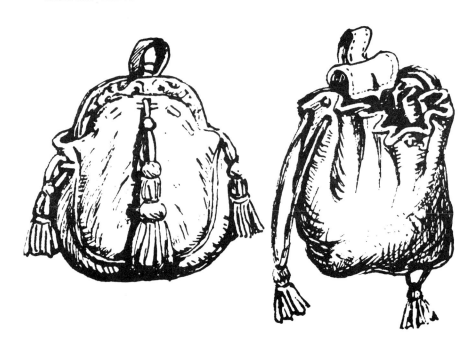

Barley Bree

> We arena fu', we're no that fu',
> Just a drappie in our e'e,
> The cock may craw, the day may daw,
> But aye we'll taste the barley bree.

(Burns)

Barley 'Bree' — beer.

Perhaps a word about barley and Scotland is in order here. Barley, oats and pease are the chief Scottish grains of the past, whether in the form of bannocks, scones or cakes. The cream of the oats, called 'sowens', was used for cosmetic purposes, and, of course, the fermented barley had a special place.

Froissart, the fourteenth century historian, writes of the Scottish soldiery: 'Under the flaps of his saddle, each man carries a broad plate of metal; behind the saddle, a little bag of oatmeal: When they have eaten too much of the sodden flesh, and their stomach appears weak and empty, they place this plate over the fire, mix with water their oatmeal, and when the plate is heated, they put a little of the paste upon it, and make a thin cake, like a cracknel or biscuit, which they eat to warm their stomachs: it is therefore no wonder that they perform a longer day's march than other solders.'

Which recalls the old lines:

> Bannocks o' bere meal
> Bannocks o' barley,
> Here's to the Hielandman's
> Bannocks o' barley

And Burns' noble commentary:

> Leeze me on thee, John Barleycorn,
>   Thou king o' grain!
> On thee auld Scotland chaws her cood
> In souple scones, the wale o' food.

For the traditional recipes, the reader should refer to F. Marian McNeill's *The Scots Kitchen*.

The tune *Barley Cakes*, to which the dance Barley Bree is set by the R.S.C.D.S., was first published by Bremner.

The Birks of Abergeldie

Abergeldie is a village on Deeside near Ballater. Birches still grow there is profusion on the slopes of the gloriously coloured hills that constitute the Braes of Mar. This is a countryside rich in song and story and the nursing ground of some of the greatest exponents of Scottish dance music. It takes nothing away from the many fiddlers who could call this region their home, to say that J. Scott Skinner was the greatest of them all.

The lively tune, *Birks of Abergeldie*, was printed by the celebrated English music publisher, John Playford, in his *Dancing Master* (1652) under the title of *A Scotch Ayre*. The words of the ballad which have come down to us are:

> Bonny lassie, will ye go, will ye go, will ye go.
> Bonny lassie, will ye go to the Birks o' Abergeldie?
> Ye shall get a gown of silk, a gown of silk, a gown of silk.
> Ye shall get a gown of silk, and a coat of calimancoe.
>
> Na, kind sir, I dare nae gang, I dare nae gang, I dare nae gang.
> Na, kind sir, I dare nae gang. My minnie she'll be angry:
> Sair, sair wad she flyte, wad she flyte, wad she flyte,
> Sair, sair wad she flyte, and sair wad she ban me.

This song was known to Burns, and when he stood by the Falls of Aberfeldy, near Moness in Perthshire, in the course of his tour of the Highlands in September 1787, the similarity of the name probably brought the old song to mind and suggested a new version which he now composed — *The Birks of Aberfeldy*:

> Bonny lassie, will ye go, will ye go, will ye go,
> Bonny lassie, will ye go to the Birks of Aberfeldy.
> Summer blinks on flowery braes,
> And o'er the crystal streamlets plays;
> Come let us spend the lightsome days
> In the birks of Aberfeldy.

40

The Birks of Invermay

The 'birches' of Invermay, a district in Perthshire at the junction of the river May with the Earn. The beautiful tune which bears this title was first published in the Orpheus Caledonius as *The Birks of Endermay*. This spelling is followed in some other eighteenth century collections, and Bremner has '*Invermay*' in the title of the song and '*Endermay*' in the title of the tune! (First Song Collection).

There is no locality known as 'Endermay' although there is a River Ender in Blair Atholl, and this has given rise to some questionings in the past. Robert Chambers, however, a noted early nineteenth century author and Scottish antiquarian, has observed: 'Ender is merely a corruption of Inver or Inner. The people of Peebles, in my young days, always spoke of Henderleithen, not Innerleithen', and this is the most acceptable explanation.

As usual with the better Scottish airs, more than one set of verses are extant. The first, however, are those due to David Malloch (or Mallet) (1705-65), who was born in Perthshire and rose from the humble station of janitor of the Edinburgh High School to a position of consequence in the literary circles of London. Unfortunately, he procured much of his progress and success at the expense of honour and was much despised in London for his self-seeking expediency. On his side he had to overcome the disadvantage of his background.

No matter, Malloch is a very minor poet who would escape our notice entirely were it not for this song. It can hardly be claimed that he has written an ideal setting, but no one has produced a better:

> The smiling morn, the breathing spring,
> Invite the tuneful birds to sing;
> And while they warble from each spray,
> Love melts the universal lay.
> Let us, *Amanda*, timely wise,
> Like them, improve the hour that flies;
> And in soft raptures waste the day
> Among the birks of Invermay.

> For soon the winter of the year,
> And age, life's winter, will appear;
> At this thy living bloom will fade,
> As that will strip the verdant shade.
> Our taste of pleasure then is o'er,
> The feathered songsters are no more;
> And when they drop, and we decay,
> Adieu the birks of Invermay!

The Country Dance *Blue Bonnets* published by the R.S.C.D.S. was collected in Perthshire. The tune is a set of a brisk 6/8 march known as *Lesley's March*. General Lesley lived in the seventeenth century, and after serving with distinction in the 'German Wars' as one of Gustavus Adolphus' commanders, he returned to Scotland to lead the Covenanting army against Cromwell's Ironsides. That he was defeated at Dunbar cannot be attributed to his generalship as he was not permitted to exercise undisputed authority over his somewhat factious forces. The march is a good one and is reproduced in Watts' *Musical Miscellany* (1731) and Oswald's *Second Collection* (1755).

A version of this tune is published in Gow's *Second Collection* as *Duplin House* and this seems to be the prototype of later versions, one of which was fitted to Sir Walter Scott's rousing poem of Border romance:

> March, march, Ettrick and Teviotdale
> Why, my lads, dinna ye march forward in order
> March, march, Eskdale and Liddesdale,
> All the blue bonnets are over the border.

This version of General Lesley's March, then, acquired the name *Blue Bonnets over the Border* from Scott's words, and hence the name of our Country Dance to this tune.

It is something of a coincidence that a tune *Blue Bonnets* in common time, very different from the above, appears in the same Oswald collection that contains Lesley's March, but its earliest appearance is in Mrs. Crockat's MS. (1709). Burns wrote words to this tune, not one of his best efforts by any means, but in this the theme of the tune, *Blue Bonnets*, plays no part, unless Burns associated it with a lady's bonnet.

The common bonnet worn by males in Scotland was of dark blue cloth with a band round the head which was, in the Highlands, sometimes striped red and white. In the Highlands, the superior ranks added a feather attached to the front by a crest, as is often seen in eighteenth century portraits of Highland chiefs, the lower ranks perhaps a sprig of heather or the like instead of a feather if a bonnet was worn at all. The same bonnet was worn in the Lowlands; a form of it was called a 'Kilmarnock Bonnet', no doubt because it was a product of the weavers of that town. This style of bonnet — to which Tam o' Shanter of Burn's poem gave his name — the 'Tammy'. Although dark blue was the familiar shade, russet was not uncommon.

Niel Gow with his blue bonnet

Although this style of bonnet could still be found worn occasionally in rural Scotland and fishing villages in the early years
of the twentieth century, it gradually disappeared from common
use during the previous century, giving way to the mass-produced
styles of cap which became common to the British Isles. The
military retained the old style of loose 'tammy' in certain regiments until recent years, although its colour was no longer blue.

In the seventeenth and eighteenth centuries, the 'Blue Bonnets' were the Scots.

Bonnie Breist Knot

> Hey the bonnie, how the bonnie,
> Hey the bonnie breist-knots!
> Tight and bonnie were they a'
> When they got on their breist-knots.

The 'breist (breast) knot' was a ribbon bow attached to the low neck of a lady's gown, and was very fashionable in the eighteenth century. A tune and words from North-East Scotland were contributed to Johnson's *Musical Museum* by an anonymous correspondent. Why anonymous?

> Hey the bonny, hey the bonny,
> O the bonny breist knots;
> Tight and bonny were they a',
> When they got on their breist knots.
>
> There was a bridal in this town,
> And till't the lasses a' were boun',
> With mankie facings on their gown,
> And some of them had breist knots.
>
> Hey the bonny, etc.

The Country Dance of this name was taken from Walsh's *Caledonian Country Dances* (*c.* 1754) and set by the R.S.C.D.S. to another tune to which John Sinclair composed a song of the same name in the first half of the nineteenth century. It is a Reel, although the R.S.C.D.S. suggests (S.C.D., Book 10, 1952 edn.) that it be performed in the Strathspey style ('Strathspey time').

Bonnie Kate of Aberdeen

The song *Kate of Aberdeen* which appears in Johnson's *Museum* was a contemporary creation. The words by John Cunningham, player, or entertainer as we might call him now; the music by Jonathan Battishill, an Englishman. Cunningham was born in Dublin in 1729. His song was published about the year 1766, the dance we are here considering was published by Thompson around 1760. It is possible, indeed likely, that Cunningham's song was the inspiration of the dance.

44

The R.S.C.D.S. has set it to a different principal tune, however, *Cropie's Strathspey*, composed by Peter Milne the early mentor and benefactor of J. Scott Skinner.

Alexander Jaffray writes that 'Kate of Aberdeen' was Miss Kitty Douglas, a celebrated beauty in Aberdeen Society. He very much admired her, but she married a Captain Mercer of the 49th regiment who was something of a minor poet. Jaffray was born in 1755, however, and if Miss Douglas was indeed the heroine of the song, she must have been over ten years Jaffray's senior. It seems much more likely that Miss Douglas received her sobriquet from the title of the song; but there is no doubt Cunningham's words and Miss Douglas are contemporaneous.

Bonniest Lass in all the World

The song of this name was first published in the *Orpheus Caledonius* in 1725. The name of its object is denied us.

Braes of Atholl
    of Busby
    of Tulliemet
    of Breadalbane

Brae = hill slope.

Atholl — The most northern district of Perthshire. It is, of course, in the heart of the Central Highlands and was once, and may be again, a region of great forests. Blair Atholl is a name giving a hint to this, as the word *blair* had the original implication of a 'place cleared of forest' — Blair Castle is the seat of the Duke of Atholl.

The reel, *Braes of Atholl*, was first published by Bremner.

Busby — A district in Renfrewshire.

Tulliemet (or Tullymet) — a district in Perthshire. The name probably means 'boundary hills' (Tully — Tulloch). The Strathspey *Braes of Tullymet* was first published in Stewart's *Collection* (eighteenth century).

Breadalbane — The 'heights of Alba', Alba being an early name for the Scottish mainland. Breadalbane is a district of Perthshire, on the south-east boundary of Atholl.

The Bumpkin or *Ninesome Reel*

The tune which appears as *Country Bumpkin* in some eighteenth century publications is best known to-day as 'bee-baw-babbity', a refrain which comes from its very old association with the cushion dance known as *Babbity Bowster* (Bab = 'bob' or 'bow' at the bolster). But there was also a form of ninesome reel danced to it at that time, which, like *Babbity Bowster*, was a finishing dance. The Gows used the Northumbrian jig *Elsie Marley* for this dance and it is essentially their version of the dance published in *The Complete Repository, pt. 4*, which the R.S.C.D.S. reproduces in *Book II*, with the alternative ending of three more men joining in to form three foursome reels.

The name 'Country Bumpkin' comes from verses set to the tune of the Scots *Babbity Bowster* in an eighteenth century English ballad opera, beginning:

> A country bumpkin who trees did grub,
> A vicar who used the pulpit to drub,
> etc.

The air was sufficiently popular to be included in four other English ballad operas, and, of course, is one of these tunes which has a touch of immortality about it.

Ca' the Yowes tae the Knowes

The 'yowes' — 'ewes', 'knowes' — 'knolls'. The shepherd lad and a lass and a beautiful, haunting air, which can only be ruined by pressing it into the mould of a dance tune. Hence the R.S.C.-D.S. has set the dance of this name to another tune. The original air is obviously Gaelic in origin and comprises only one strain of 8-bars. The chorus is the best of both the original verses and the verses contributed by Burns:

> Ca' the yowes tae the knowes,
> Ca' them whaur the heather growes,
> Ca' them whaur the burnie rowes,
> My bonnie dearie.

Burns picked up this song in 1787, from a Rev. Mr. Clunie whom he was visiting in the company of Stephen Clarke the Edinburgh organist who, Burns tells us, took down the song at his request. The bard passed on the modified original verses to Johnson for the *Museum* and composed a different set for Thomson's *Collection*. I think the former are preferable.

Cadgers in the Canongate

A 'cadger' was a hired carrier of goods. He carried his pack on his back or strapped it to his horse — a 'pack-horse' as we would call it. Although Scotsmen were to make a notable contribution to the engineering of road building in the late eighteenth century, to which the name of Macadam bears testimony, most roads prior to that time were hardly fit to support a cart or carriage. The pack-horse and the packman could carry loads with greater ease along them, although in wet weather, even they were balked by the deep ruts of mire, the stones and the pools of water. Farmers conveyed their oats and barley to market on horseback requiring many trips to transport their complete load.

The Canongate is the most celebrated of Edinburgh's historic streets. Famous personalities or characters of Scotland's story once lived in its tall 'lands', or 'flats' as we would call them to-day, and trod its length through the seven centuries of its existence. It is quite futile to try to name them all; the kings, the queens, the divines, the lords, the merchants, the professors and even the criminals.

The word 'gate' is the Germanic word for road, or way, and the Canongate has taken its name from the fact that it was the 'way' from the walled town clustered on the castle rock down the long slope to the Augustinian abbey of the Holyrood, established in 1128. Many of the historic apartments, closes and hallowed stones along this street remain, and after seeing some recent years of decay, have been most felicitously restored.

The city walls of Edinburgh were built in the fifteenth century, and the great stone portal opening the wall on to the Canongate was called the Netherbow Port.

The Canongate, Edinburgh

When the Edinburgh dance *Assembly* was inaugurated in 1723, 'in the great hall in Patrick Steil's Close', the event was lauded by those of a moderate or liberal taste as a triumph for refinement, while the more puritanically devout regarded it, as did Patrick Walker, as a 'common evil'. Patrick, a prominent minister and writer on the 'troubles' of the Kirk, could not understand how any one who had ever known what it was to bend a knee in prayer 'durst crook a hough to fyke and fling at a piper's and fiddler's springs'. He was thankful that in his 'dancing days' the seriousness of the Covenanting troubles and the horrors awaiting him if brought to account by his Kirk's persecutors, stopped 'the lightness' of his head and 'the wantonness' of his feet. He deplored the dilution of religious fervour of his time and the open profanation of the Lord's Day — 'The throng streets, particularly fields, milkhouses, ale-houses in and about sinful Edinburgh . . . many going to the fields before sermons, and after sermons multitudes go to their walks.'

To Patrick, and even to many others who were somewhat less fervent, Richard Cameron, who fell a martyr at Airmoss, near the water of Ayr, in July 1680, was no less than a saint. No wonder Patrick objected to the use of the *Cameron March* or *Cameronian Rant* as a dance tune, or perhaps even to the naming of any secular tune after the revered Cameron or his followers.

Richard Cameron was the greatest of the field preachers during that period under Charles II when hundreds of the people of the southern counties of Scotland followed their deposed ministers out of the church to prohibited services in moorland or hill-top, under circumstances of great danger and consequently of high exultation. The source of the trouble was the desire of the King to establish episcopacy in the Church of Scotland, as his father, Charles I and his grandfather James VI had desired before him. The consequences to Charles I should have been warning enough; but Charles II's privy councillors were for enforcement, so the dragoons went out and the 'Killing time' entered the pages of history.

Richard Cameron was born in Falkland in Fife about the year 1648 and graduated M.A. at St. Andrews, 1662. On returning from a period in exile at Rotterdam, he led an assembly of the most devout at the Market Cross at Sanquhar in Ayrshire, June 22, 1680, and issued an impassioned declaration for the deposing of the King. When, a month later, Cameron and his sixty or so men were set upon by troopers, he was one of those left dead upon the heath; but his head and hands were carried to Edinburgh to win the 5000 marks set on him, dead or alive, and so he entered the ranks of the immortals in the lore of the struggles of the Presbyterian Kirk in Scotland.

Much can be said of these struggles and their effects on Scotland. To be fair to Charles II, we must acknowledge that he expressed doubts about the wisdom of the methods recommended and instigated by his privy councillors. His Roman Catholic brother, as Duke of York, offered pardon to some of the 'poor demented creatures' who were about to be executed in Edinburgh, while he was resident there in 1681, if they would but utter the words 'God save the King'. This they refused to do, because of their conception of the implications of the phrase.

Both sides, or rather it should be said *all* sides — for there were more than two — allowed little room for compromise. It was an intolerant age, and principles were to be imposed as well as defended. Here was heroism, there cruelty, and Christian charity scarcely recognized.

The Cameronians, chiefly formed in the counties of Lanark, Dumfries and Kirkcudbright, were most uncompromising of all — 'the Antipopish, Antiprelatic, Antierastian, Antisectarian, True Presbyterian Church of Scotland', as they described themselves. They objected to what they called the 'land-ruining, God-provoking, soul-destroying, and posterity-ensnaring-and-enslaving Union' with England in 1707, and in this they touch upon the Scottish religious patriotism which is a characteristic of the whole episode.

A regiment was raised in the time of William of Orange, members of which carried a bible in their pouch, and this became known as the *Cameronians*, a regiment which existed into recent times until it became the *Scottish Rifles*.

The Tune *Cameronian March, Reel or Rant* — it appears under all three names — was also known as *Shirra Muir* on account of its being used as a setting for a humorous song, or songs, about that celebrated battle between the Government forces under Argyll and the rebel Jacobites under the Earl of Mar, in 1715. That celebrated encounter was so confused that each side presumed itself the victor:

There's some say that we wan,
Some say that they wan,
And some say that nane wan at a', man:
But one thing I'm sure,
That at Sherramuir,

A battle there was, that I saw, man:
And we ran, and they ran,
And they ran, and we ran,
And we ran, and they ran awa', man.

50

Cauld Kail

Kail or kale is the vegetable colewort, sometimes called 'greens' in England. It grows on a stalk, has large crinkly leaves and is of the cabbage family. Kail is usually used in broth, and often a vegetable soup containing kail was called kail-broth or simply 'kail'. Cold kail would be such a broth that had cooled and had lost its savour. Hence the familiar Scottish saying with reference to the restoration of old ideas or practices which have seen their day — 'cauld kail het again' (cold kail re-heated!).

The tune is of the class we call 'Strathspey' and takes its name, as is usual when a tune becomes the vehicle of a song, from the verses associated with it. These, as collected by the eighteenth century collector David Herd are:

> Cauld kail in Aberdeen,
> And castocks in Strabogie,
> But yet I fear they'll cook o'er soon,
> And never warm the cogie.
> The lassies about Bogie gicht
> Their limbs, they are sae clean and tight,
> That if they were but girded right,
> They'll dance the reel of Bogie.
>
> Wow, Aberdeen, what did you mean,
> Sae young a maid to woo sir?
> I'm sure it was nae joke to her,
> Whate'er it was to you, sir;
> For lasses now are no sae blate
> But they ken auld folk's out o' date,
> And better playfare can they get
> Than castocks in Strabogie.

A 'castock' is the stalk of the cabbage or kail and a 'cog' was a wooden vessel or bowl. With this knowledge we can interpret the first lines of the above as:

> Cold kail in Aberdeen
> And cabbage stalks in Strathbogie
> But yet I fear they'll cook to soon,
> And never warm the bowl.

The point of the satire is revealed in the second verse, an old man, apparently an Earl of Aberdeen, has been trying to woo a young maid.

51

The 'reel of Bogie' in the above is a euphemism for amorous activity. The Bogie is a river in Aberdeenshire which is often mentioned in song and story. Its valley, Strathbogie, is particularly fertile and beautiful.

The tune *Cauld Kail* has been a favourite of song writers, and consequently several sets of verses are now extant. These uniformly transform it into a humorous toper's song, e.g.

> There's cauld kail in Aberdeen
> And castocks in Strabogie,
> Where ilka man maun hae his lass
> But I maun hae my coggie.

The 'coggie' here is a cog of ale.

In Johnson's *Musical Museum*, the words selected were written by the Duke of Gordon — a very characteristic hobby of Scotland's nobility in the eighteenth century.

The dance *Cauld Kail* is a medley, that is, Strathspey followed by Reel, in its most common form. Jig followed by reel was another musical combination called 'medley' at the end of the eighteenth century, but never strathspey and jig.

Circassian Circle

This dance is a survivor of a 'round the room' class of dance which grew in popularity in the late nineteenth century, particularly in English ballrooms. It is not a Country Dance.

Cold and Raw

The tune of this name was one of those Scottish tunes which became great favourites in England during the seventeenth and eighteenth centuries and has a special place in history on account of its being asked for by Queen Mary, wife of William of Orange, at a private command performance largely devoted to the music of the great Henry Purcell. Hawkins tells us that the Queen had begun to tire of the recital and that Purcell was a little chagrined to have to sit idle at the harpsichord while the celebrated Mrs. Hunt accompanied herself in a performance of the rude old Scottish ballad, apparently preferred to his own compositions. This occurred in the year 1691.

52

For the Queen's birthday of the following year, however, Purcell composed an air to the words 'May her bright example chase vice in troops out of the land' to which *Cold and Raw* provides the bass.

The original refrain began:

> Cold and raw the wind does blaw
> Up in the mornin' early.

It is characteristic of Scottish song to begin with the refrain.

Burns composed a revision of the song of which the refrain is now the better known:

> Up in the mornin's no for me
> Up in the mornin' early,
> When a' the hills are cover'd wi' snaw,
> I'm sure it is winter fairly.

The picture this draws for Scottish minds is one of crisp clear mornings, trees gaunt and bare, ploughed fields stretching their hard frozen furrows to the undulating hedgerows fringed with hoar, clumsy trains of rooks circling their lofty refuge in the 'planting' near the grey farm house, the hills elegant in new-laundered white. The 'hand folded air' chilling the nostrils and faint wraiths rising from the cattle in their stibble pasture. The sun weak and low down and the puddles and dubs glazed with thin ice.

There are parts of the world where the cold is iron-fisted, tree-bursting, but in Scotland it has a softer touch, though moist and murky much of the time and tempestuous too, with rain more often than snow, it is not long before the first snowdrops appear and primroses bloom as the hawthorn hedgerows whisper a hint of Spring.

It is a striking fact that Scottish poets, particularly those using the Teutonic language, have been markedly fascinated with Winter before all the seasons. It is the time of the long night, of course, and the 'hamely fireside clime', with its ancient emphasis on 'the social bowl' exuding an irresistible contrast to the dark, and the death of Nature outside.

> The wind made wave the reid weed on the dyke;
> Bedovin in donkis deep was every syk;
> Owre craggis, and the front of rockis seir,
> Hang great ice-shoklis lang as ony spear;
> The grund stude barrand, widderit, dosk and grey,
> Herbis, flouris, and grasses wallowit away;

In this congealit season sharp and chill,
The caller air penetrative and pure,
Dasing the blood in every creature,
Made seek warm stovis, and bien firis hot,
In double garment clad and wylie-coat,
With michty drink, and meatis comfortive,
Agane the stormy winter for to strive.

Gavin Douglas (1475-1522)
Prologue to Book VII, Aeneid

Into thir dark and drublie dayis,
When sable all the heaven arrayis,
   With misty vapouris, cludis and skyis,
   Nature all courage me denyis
Of sangis, ballattis, and of playis.

William Dunbar (1460-1530)

When hailstanes drive wi' bitter skyte,
And infant frosts begin to bite,
   In hoary cranreuch drest;

While winds frae off Ben Lomond blaw,
And bar the doors wi' driving snaw,
   And hing us owre the ingle.

Burns (1759-1796)

It was a wild black nicht,
But o' the win's roar we
Kept juist eneuch tae hear our herts beat
Ower it triumphantly.

It was a wild black nicht,
But o' the Earth we
Kept juist eneuch underneath us tae ken
That a warl used tae be.

Hugh MacDiarmid

Or just to return to *Cold and Raw:*

Cauld blaws the wind frae east to west,
   The drift is driving fairly;
Sae loud and shill's I hear the blast,
   I'm sure it's winter fairly.

The birds sit chittering in the thorn,
   A' day they fare but sparsely;
And lang's the night frae e'en to morn,
   I'm sure it's winter fairly.

Corn Rigs

The word 'rig' used here is probably from the 'run-rig' system of farming referred to later under 'Lea Rig'. Under this system, the fields were divided among a number of joint tenants in the form of strips or 'rigs'. In Scotland, the word 'corn' is used particularly of oats, but often as a generic term for grain. In North America, of course, maize is called 'corn'; it is a crop unfamiliar in the British Isles.

The tune, *Corn Rigs*, is a characteristic Scottish double hornpipe, and takes its name from the song. The oldest surviving refrain of which runs as follows:

> O corn rigs and rye rigs,
> And corn rigs are bonnie,
> And gin ye meet a bonnie lass
> Prin up her cockernony.

(*prin* — pin; *cockernony* — the gathering of a woman's hair into the 'snood' or fillet.)

Burns, however, transmuted it into its best-known form. It is one of the most loved of Scottish Lowland songs, it haunts the imagination and conjures images of undulating fields of ripe grain waving in the wind or shimmering in the silver light of the moon, ready for harvest, all but one anxiety past, and that removed only when the last sheaf is wound into the elaborate mystic symbol of the harvest goddess, and the barn is prepared for the kirn:

It fell upon a Lammas nicht,
  When corn rigs are bonnie,
Beneath the moon's unclouded light,
  I held awa to Annie:
The time flew by, wi' tentless heed,
  Till, 'tween the late and early,
Wi' sma' persuasion she agreed
  To see me thro' the barley.

Chorus:
Corn rigs an' barley rigs,
  An' corn rigs are bonnie:
I'll ne'er forget that happy nicht,
  Amang the rigs wi' Annie.

The Sky was blue, the wind was still,
  The moon was shining clearly;
I set her down, wi' right good will,
  Amang the rigs o' barley:
I kent her hert was a' my ain;
  I loved her most sincerely;
I kissed her owre and owre again,
  Amang the rigs o' barley.

I hae been blythe wi' comrades dear;
  I hae been merry drinking;
I hae been joyfu' gath'rin' gear;
  I hae been happy thinking:
But a' the pleasures e'er I saw,
  Tho' three times doubled fairly,
That happy nicht was worth them a',
  Amang the rigs o' barley.

55

The Countess of Crawford's Reel

The identity of this Countess of Crawford hinges, of course, upon the date of composition of the Reel of that name to which Walsh published the figures of the Country Dance. There was no Countess of Crawford from early in the eighteenth century until December 1755, with the exception of a seven-month period in 1747. Walsh's dance was published in 1754. It seems most probable then that the Reel and possibly also the dance, were composed in honour of Lady Jane Murray, daughter of the Duke of Atholl, who, in 1747, at the tender age of sixteen eloped with that battle-scarred warrior of more than twice her age, the Twentieth Earl of Crawford. Her premature death of a fever at Utrecht, but seven months later, was very tragic.

This Earl of Crawford was a famous mercenary soldier who saw extensive military service for different imperial powers in Europe, including Russia, from about 1733 until the '45 when he was recalled from the British Army in France (where it had suffered a reverse at Fontenoy) to take a command under the Prince of Hesse who had brought over 6000 of his men to fight for his father-in-law, George II, against Prince Charles.

It seems likely that Lord Crawford first met Lady Jane while he was with the Duke of Atholl at Dunkeld House at the time the family house at Blair Atholl was being besieged by a detachment of the Highland army under his brother, Lord George Murray. At this time, Lord George invited the Prince of Hesse to enter into a cartel for the exchange of prisoners, a proposal which met with the Prince's approval. Cumberland, however, was furious at his father's being referred to as 'the Elector of Hanover' in the correspondence and refused to consider it. The Prince of Hesse, and consequently the Earl of Crawford, took no further active part in the campaign, the prince protesting that he was 'not enough interested in the quarrel between the Houses of Stuart and Hanover' to sacrifice his subjects' lives in 'combatting with men driven to despair'.

The Earl's education was exceptionally broad and included a period at the French military academy in the 1720's, where he was noted for his distinguished horsemanship (even the Cossacks were impressed), fencing and *dancing*.

The R.S.C.D.S. has abandoned the original tune, however, in favour of the Strathspey *Lady Elizabeth Lindsay*, but the dance retains the old name with its recollections of Crawford and the memory of his spirited young wife.

56

Crieff Fair

Crieff, strategically situated at the openings in the Grampian fringe to bonnie Stratherne and the Perthshire Highlands, spread on a southern slope and surrounded by wooded hills, vistas of mountains and intersecting burns and rivers, was once known as the Montpelier of Scotland. Agricola and his Roman legionaries camped in this region, but we do not know what they thought of it. They had a taste for the therapeutic value of spring water but it is probably only a coincidence that Nature has provided this near-by in Lower Stratherne.

In the early years of the nineteenth century, every one in Crieff and its neighbourhood spoke both Gaelic and English, about the farthest remaining penetration of Gaelic into the Lowlands at that time. There are few natives of this region who consciously know a word of Gaelic to-day, and the linguistic history of the place explains why the Scoto-Saxon tongue has no claim on its sentiment. The Anglo-Saxon dialect therefore is now the most familiar there as in other parts of the Highlands which have lost their native tongue.

The salubrity of Crieff attracted the more wealthy holiday-makers and Hall complains in 1804 of the excessive prices which this occasioned.

More relevant to our subject, however, is the fair or 'tryst' which was annually held at Crieff. This was the most important market of the Highland stock-raiser's year, well into the eighteenth century. After which time, for some reason, the honour passed to Falkirk, farther south. Here the English graziers foregathered to purchase the droves of black cattle brought down from the glens and straths of the north and west. Highland gentlemen of long pedigree, we are told by a traveller in 1729, could be seen there selling their oxen, 'mightily civil-dressed in their slashed waist-coats, trousings and blue bonnets, with their poniards and broad-swords, all speaking Irish'. Such was Crieff Fair.

Dance assemblies at Crieff, in the late eighteenth century, were conducted in the large hall in the old Drummond Arms Inn.

Crookit Horned Ewie, The

The 'Ewie wi' the Crookit Horn' is a euphemism for a whisky still.

> The Ewie wi' the crookit horn,
> Wha had kent her might have sworn,
> Sic a ewe was never born
> Hereabouts, not far awa'.
>
> A better or a thriftier beast,
> Nae honest man could weel hae wist,
> For, silly thing, she never mist
> To hae, ilk year, a lamb or twa.
>
> The first she had I gae to Jock,
> To be to him a kind o' stock,
> And now the laddie has a flock
> O' mair nor thirty head ava.

The above chorus and two verses are from the Rev. John Skinner's long and humorous poem on the theme. The tune, a reel, is a famous one originally entitled *Carron's Reel*. It is said that this was the tune which Niel Gow played when he won the fiddling competition which first brought him to more general notice.

Although whisky had long been a common drink in the Scottish Highlands, it did not make significant inroads into the Lowlands until after about 1750. By 1778, however, Edinburgh was estimated to harbour 400 unlicensed stills, and 2000 licensed alehouses retailing spirits to 75,000 inhabitants! Similar statistics could be furnished for most towns and country villages at this time. If illicit stills could thrive in Edinburgh, what was the situation in the lonely straths and wild parts of the Highlands?

After the union with England, smuggling of silks, tea, cambric, brandy and wine from the Continent became a thriving business. County magnates, magistrates, farmers, craftsmen of all kinds and even the lairds themselves, participated in the traffic. The excise imposed by the 'English' parliament was fair game. Illicit distillers were as much respected as smugglers. The story is told of a minister in Roseneath, on the Clyde, remonstrating with an illicit distiller in his parish; the distiller felt not a little offended and replied. 'I alloo nae sweerin' in the still, everything's dune decently and in order. I canna see ony harm in't.' (*Story's Life Story of Roseneath*, p.49.)

The clergy elsewhere were not always so censorious. One traveller writes in 1807: 'It is a shame that the clergy in the Shetland and Orkney Isles should so often wink at their churches being made depositories of smuggled goods, chiefly foreign spirits'. (Hall, *Travels in Scotland* 1807, pp.ii, 517.)

The consumption of ale, hitherto the most popular drink, declined as the eighteenth century progressed, while the consumption of whisky increased at a fantastic rate.

In the Highlands, he was a very poor man who was ever without whisky with which to share a social dram. No innkeeper or host would permit a guest to leave, no matter the time of day, without placing before him a tray with bottle or bottles, glasses and some cake, for a *deoch an dorus*, 'a drink at the door' — a stirrup cup. Even tradesmen or messengers calling at the big houses on the Highland estates could always be sure of a dram. It was the essential ingredient of those respected ceremonies of hospitality so dear to the Highlander, of which many traces survive to this day.

It is a striking fact that a glass of whisky was so much an accepted part of life in Scotland that it was not thought out of place even in the hand of a minister of the gospel. Indeed it was much more common for ministers to warn their flocks against the evils of excessive banqueting, singing of 'profane sangis' and dancing at weddings than to condemn the ale drinking which caused most of the trouble, if trouble there was.

The growth of modern industrial society produced circumstances which brought into focus whisky as a social evil, and temperance became an issue, as it had never been in previous times. Superior communications and depopulation led to the disappearance of the 'ewies wi' the crookit horns', yet he would be a bold man who would say that the breed is extinct.

Dainty Davie

The tune *Dainty Davie* was well known in the seventeenth century and appeared in print in Playford's *Dancing Master 7th edn.* (1680), p.293. Many verses have been set to it, notably Ramsay's 'Lucky Nancy' and Burns' 'There was a lad was born in Kyle'. To confuse matters, the Burns song is almost always published now to a different, but similar tune which he used for another lyric, *O an ye were dead, gudeman.* Dick attributes this fashion to John Templeton, a Scottish tenor with the Italian Opera, who popularized it. There is no doubt about its suitability.

A set of verses current in the countryside and recorded by the collector, David Herd (1776) (II.215) runs as follows:

> It was in and through the window broads,
> And all the tirliewirlies o'd:
> The sweetest kiss that e'er I got
> Was from my Dainty Davie.
>
> Chorus:
> O leeze me on your curly pow,
> Dainty Davie, Dainty Davie,
> Leeze me on your curly pow,
> My ain dainty Davie.
>
> It was down amang my daddy's pease,
> And underneath the cherry trees:
> O there he kist me as he pleas'd,
> For he was mine ain dear Davie.
>
> When he was chased by a dragoon,
> Into my bed he was laid down,
> I thought him wordy o' his room,
> And he's aye my dainty Davie.

Herd states in a footnote that the song 'was made upon Mess David Williamson, on getting with child the Lady Cherrytree's daughter, while the soldiers were searching the house to apprehend him for a rebel'.

The story goes that David Williamson, a preacher at the time of the Covenanting troubles, being pursued by a troop of Dalzell's dragoons, sought refuge in the house of Cherrytrees, where Lady Cherrytrees hit upon the ingenious artifice of putting him into a bed beside her daughter. The Reverend David gave substance to the tale when he married Miss Cherrytrees, and it is likely as the song implies, that he was already her suitor when he took refuge in her bed. Whatever the facts, the old song was modified to allude to this incident, and pasquils were composed on it then and later.

The ministry of the Rev. David Williamson was associated with Kirk o' Shotts and Aberdeen, and Woodrow, the historian of the Scottish Kirk, describes an incident in which a 'crazy man' danced and sang *Dainty Davie* before the minister, one Sunday, while he was on his way to the Church in Aberdeen. It is suggested by some that this is the incident which gave rise to his soubriquet but it is just as likely that the soubriquet inspired the incident.

It is recorded, however, that 'Dainty Davie' married and buried six wives, and a seventh who buried him — in 1706. He did not outlive his former and valiant mother-in-law, however, as a notice appears in the *Edinburgh Courier*, January 1729, that the Lady Cherrytrees had died in the 104th year of her age. (See Chambers, *Dom. Annals of Scotland v.III.*)

Dalkeith Strathspey

Dalkeith, a town near Edinburgh, seat of the Duke of Buccleuch, chief of the Border family of Scott. The Duke's eldest son assumes the title of Earl of Dalkeith.

Dashing White Sergeant

The origin of this title is not to be found in Scotland, although the dance has long been popular there. It comes from the theatrical lyric composed by General Burgoyne, about the girl who wishes to dress as a soldier and follow her 'beau' in the ranks:

> If I had a beau
> For a soldier who'd go,
> Do you think I'd say no?
> No, not I!
> When his red coat I saw,
> Not a tear would it draw,
> But I'd give him eclat for his bravery!
>> If an army of amazons e'er came in play,
>> As a dashing white sergeant I'd march away.

General Burgoyne had the misfortune to be obliged to surrender his outnumbered forces at Saratoga in 1777, and thus inadvertantly decide the course of the American War of Independence — which is no small distinction, one may say.

The dance, however, belongs to the latter half of the nineteenth century. It involves the basic sequence of set and reel of the threesome *Scotch Reel*, with partners turned by taking hands as in the Country Dance. It also involves a progression round the room which relates it to what were called Swedish Country Dances. The tune was composed by Henry Bishop, the popular 'drawing room' composer of the early nineteenth century, whose *Home Sweet Home* is still well known, and whose *Lo Hear the Gentle Lark* was once beloved of *coloratura* sopranos.

De'il Among the Tailors

An old game of this name was once to be seen, as Strutt tells us, (*Sports and Pastimes of the English People*, London, 1876 .) 'at low public houses, where many idle people resort and play it for beer and trifling stakes of money . . . it consists of nine small pins placed like skittles in the midst of a circular board, surrounded by a ledge with a small recess on one side, in which a peg-top is set up by means of a string drawn through a crevice in the recess; the top when loosed spins about among the pins and beats some, or all of them, down before its motion ceases; the players at this game spin the top alternately, and he who first beats down the pins to the number of one-and-thirty is the conqueror'.

62

The Deuks Dang Ow'er My Daddie

'Deuks' has usually been identified as the Scots word for 'ducks', pronounced 'juks'. The meaning of the title, then, would be — 'the ducks knocked over my Father', which is not very logical and bears no relation to the sense of the song:

> The bairns gat out wi' an unco shout,
> The deuks dang o'er my daddie O!
> The fient-ma-care, quo' the feirrie auld wife,
> He was but a paidlin body, O!
>
> He paidles out, and he paidles in,
> And he paidles late and early O!
> This seven lang years I hae lien by his side,
> An' he is but a fushionless carlie, O!

(*feirrie* — clever; *paidlan* — to walk with short steps; *fushionless* — feeble.)

It seems much more plausible, and certainly more acceptable, that the word 'deuk' is a misspelling of 'deoch', a dram, as in the well-known Gaelic phrase *deoch an dorus*. The 'drams knocked over my Daddie' — but he 'aye was a paidlan body!'

The alternative title for this dance, in the R.S.C.D.S. collection is *Just as I was in the Morning*. This is another name given the tune in Bremner's collection. It certainly confirms our interpretation of *deuks*.

The district of Atholl, the core, one may say, of the Central Highlands, was anciently associated with the royal family of Alba (or Caledonia as the Romans called it) and later, Scotland. The 'Earldom' of Atholl was founded in the reign of King Malcolm Canmore, who succeeded Macbeth in 1056 and came into the possession of his grandson (the Third Earl). The succession has passed to the female line, owing to extinction of the male succession, a number of times in history and was forfeited and re-bestowed more than once.

The Dukedom of Atholl sprang from another family, the Murrays, said to be descended from Freskin, a Flemish settler in the twelfth century who adopted the name *de Moravia* from property in Moray, one of whose descendants acquired the lands of Tullibardine. The earldom of Atholl also fell to the Murrays in the seventeenth century and the two were combined in the Marquisate of Atholl in 1676. Marriage related the Marquis' family with most of the principal families of Europe. The Second Marquis became the First Duke of Atholl and became suspected of participation in a Jocobite conspiracy, thanks to the mischief of the Twelfth Lord Lovat who was an avowed enemy.

The Atholl Highlanders were certainly pro-Jacobite and three of the duke's sons were to distinguish themselves in that cause. His second surviving son, James, succeeded him as his eldest son, William, Marquis of Tullibardine, had been attainted and exiled for his activities in the '15 rebellion. William ('Tullibardine') was, of course, called 'Duke of Atholl' by the Jacobites. He it was who sailed with Prince Charlie and unfurled the standard at Glenfinnan in 1745. His younger brother, George, became commander-in-chief of the Prince's army. Brother James, however, designated Second Duke of Atholl, adhered to the Hanoverian cause. He was married twice, the second time to Jane Drummond, the heroine of Dr. Austen's song 'For lack of gold she left me, O!' He was succeeded in 1764 by his surviving daughter, Charlotte, who married her cousin, John, the eldest son of the gallant Lord George mentioned above. John died in 1774 and was succeeded by his eldest son, now the Fourth Duke (d. 1830) with whom Burns spent two days in 1787.

The most important retainer — from our point of view — of the Second, Third and Fourth Dukes of Atholl was the great fiddler Niel Gow (1727-1807) and there is no disputing the fertility of the province of Atholl, and those adjoining, in the production of the traditional dance music and its exponents. The tune 'The Duchess of Athole's Slipper' was composed by Niel Gow.

The Duke of Buccleuch is chief of the Border family of Scott. The family seat is Dalkeith Palace but was formerly Branxholm Castle — the 'Branxsome Ha' ' of ballad lore, which has long been a ruin:

> An' word has gaen tae the bauld Buccleugh
> In Branksome Ha' whaur that he lay . . .

There have been a number of estimable bearers of the title. The Fourth Duke was most practical in assisting Sir Walter Scott at a very difficult time and enjoyed a long correspondence with him. He also bestowed on that other Border poet, James Hogg, the 'Ettrick Shepherd', a life rent of a farm on the Braes of Yarrow, celebrated in Border rhyme.

The First Duke was a distinguished dancer, none other than the Duke of Monmouth, natural son of Charles II who married Anne, Countess of Buccleuch, in 1663. She was then twelve and he fourteen! He assumed the name of Scott and was created Duke of Buccleuch. In the way of so many distinguished gentlemen, he lost his head for leading a cause which lost — this time his own cause, that of succeeding his father to the crown in place of his father's brother James, the legitimate successor. He was joined by the Earl of Argyll in an attempt to depose James, but the rebellion failed. James was, of course, later forced to abdicate in favour of his daughter Mary.

The parting of Monmouth and his wife, Duchess of Buccleuch, was a sad and tender episode. She, however, enjoyed more favour of the King and managed to keep her estates entire for her son. She had six children and married again; this time, Lord Cornwallis, who died in 1732.

She nevertheless attempted to keep up the state of a princess of the blood, with attending pages serving her on bent knee and no one being allowed to sit in her presence. She also had a state room with a chair, or throne, under a canopy. One of her relatives described how she had dined with the Duchess at Dalkeith, and was allowed a chair only because she was a relative. The other guests had to stand during the dinner.

For those interested in the eighteenth century social life of Scotland, two celebrated hostesses stand out — Susanna, Countess of Eglintoun in the first half of the century; Jane, Duchess of Gordon, in the second half. Jane was the handsomest of the three lively daughters of Sir William Maxwell of Monreith, a dissipated man who left them in penurious circumstances in the care of their mother. As Henry Mackenzie says, 'they lived very sparingly, but kept up a good countenance and the best society' in Hyndford's Close at the bottom of Edinburgh High Street, on the south side. Anne, Countess of Balcarres, mother of a large family, lived in the same close as, later, did Sir Walter Scott's uncle, Dr. Rutherford.

It was no unfamiliar sight to see one of the Maxwell girls carrying the tea-kettle to the Fountain Well for water to make tea, and one of their relatives, in later years, told Robert Chambers, writer of *The Traditions of Edinburgh*, that the first time he saw them, Miss Jane was riding upon a sow in the street, while her sister, Miss Eglintoun, drove it along with a stick. The sow belonged to a nearby innkeeper. Such were the easy manners of the Scottish gentry in that wonderful century and such was the romping spirit of the Maxwell lassies. Who would have anticipated their distinguished role of the future and that they would be a subject of conversation two centuries later — a long time later?

The Scotch Wedding

Miss Eglintoun married Sir Thomas Wallace of Craigie, the eldest son of Mrs. Dunlop, Burns' correspondent, and the oldest sister married Mr. Fordyce, civil servant and great favourite of Lord Melville and Mr. Pitt. It was at Mr. Fordyce's house that Miss

Jane met the Duke of Gordon, author of a version of *Cauld Kail*. Later she danced with him at Comely Gardens, a poor imitation of Vauxhall, near Holyrood House, which had a short life, and so captivated him by her beauty and vivacity that he married her in 1767, when she was about eighteen.

For some years she was occupied in the raising of her family and supplying the deficiencies in her own education. This she did so well as to become very well versed in English and French literature and an Italian scholar. She loved company, dancing and music, and became a great leader of fashion and centre of social life in the North, in Edinburgh and even in London itself, where she had a Tory *salon* in her house in Pall Mall (1787-1801). While the Duchess of Devonshire led the Whig set, the Duchess of Gordon led the Tory set. Her energy was prodigious, and no name occurs more often in dedications of reels and Strathspeys and collections of these. Francis Peacock's book on dancing — the first written and published in Scotland (1805) — was dedicated to her.

Robert Burns was proud to address the Duchess as his patron and she was much charmed by him on his visit to Edinburgh in 1786 and entertained him to dinner on his visit to Castle Gordon during his Highland tour the next summer.

Her daughters, for whom the Duchess obviously gave much of herself, made august marriages: her eldest became Duchess of Richmond; another, Marchioness of Cornwallis; another, Duchess of Manchester, a fourth, Duchess of Bedford; and a fifth, Lady Sinclair. She was the butt of many cartoons in the English capital, one in particular I have seen depicts her making marriages for her daughters. Such an indefatigable socialite, particularly sustained as she was by an all-conquering Scottish 'smeddum', shared in no small degree by her sister Lady Wallace, ran the risk of satire and censure. Sir Water Scott thought she was insensitive and inconsiderate; but she obviously had the common touch which enabled her to win the hearts of her tenants in Strathspey.

In her later years, she retired to a cottage in Strathspey which she built on a farm she took from the Duke called 'Kinrara' where, it may be remembered, Elizabeth Grant recalls enjoying the frequent dances held during the summer.

It is often the penalty of those who present an aspect of gaiety and happiness under the stimulus of company and occasion, to suffer lonely periods of introspection and even melancholy. The celebrated Duchess of Gordon was doubtless of this category and showed evidence of it in what Henry Mackenzie called her 'sincere religious turn'. Who could have persuaded her that she had no need of the memorial she built for herself at Kinrara as long as Scottish dance and music lived?

The Duke is Welcome to Inverness or *Lady MacIntosh's Reel*

There is either satire or irony in the titles of this dance. The tune is *Lady MacIntosh's Reel* but Walsh renamed it *The Duke is Welcome to Inverness* in his *Caledonian Country Dances* (c. 1756). The 'Duke' in this case can only be the Duke of Cumberland whose name commands not the slightest claim to our respect. The satire or irony arises from the fact that Lady MacIntosh was a staunch supporter of Prince Charles and figured in an incident before Culloden which led to the evacuation of Inverness by Government troops under Lord Loudon. At no time could it be said that the 'Duke' was 'welcome to Inverness'.

Indeed, in 1750, a Jacobite song to the tune was actually printed (*Loyal Songs*), of which the chorus is:

> For a' that, and a' that,
> And thrice as muckle's a' that;
> He's far beyond the seas the night,
> Yet he'll be here for a' that.

There is evidence of several variants of this song gaining currency in the countryside, a licentious example being included in *The Merry Muses*. Burns, however, turned it into a song extolling the dignity and brotherhood of man:

> Is there for honest poverty
> That hings his heid, an' a' that?
> The coward slave, we pass him by --
> We daur be puir for a' that!
> For a' that, an' a' that,
> Our toils obscure, an' a' that,
> The rank is but the guinea's stamp,
> The man's the gowd for a' that.

This is one of Burns' most characteristic effusions which reveal his response to the social issues of his times and his great rhetorical gifts. He had already made a different song for the tune in his *Jolly Beggars*, beginning, 'I am a bard, of no regard'.

The tune is varied a little between one setting and another but the parent is *Lady MacIntosh's Reel*. The R.S.C.D.S. ought not to perpetuate any other title to Walsh's dance, nor should the reader.

What about Lady MacIntosh? She was born Anne Farquharson of Invercauld and was of an almost masculine temperament. She traversed the country in male dress (i.e. tartan doublet and trews) to help raise the hundred men required for her husband's captaincy in Lord Loudon's Highlanders, just before Prince Charles arrived in Moidart. When the Prince raised his standard, the gallant lady directed her energies to raising two battalions from the seventeen clans which comprise the kin of Clan Chattan, for the rebel cause. All this, it may be remarked, while Angus, her Whig husband, held a command with the opposing forces.

If we doubted her individuality, her letters, of which the following is an interesting example, would surely dissuade us:

> My Lord Douke, — The Bearer of this is a Very Pretay fellew, Brother of Mcenzie of Killcoway. He has a Company Resed for the Prince's Service, but was handered by Lord Siforth of Keray them of, which meks me geve this trobal to beg of your Grace to geve hem en ordar for resing his men. . . .

Duke is Welcome to Inverness

In the later stages of the withdrawal of the Jacobite army, Prince Charles arrived with an advance guard of Camerons at Castle Moy, seat of the Laird of MacIntosh, about ten miles from Inverness where he was hospitably received by Lady MacIntosh. Lord Loudon's army was then occupying Inverness and when news came of the arrival of the Prince, Loudon thought to capture him with a night sorty on the castle. Lady MacIntosh's mother who

69

lived in Inverness, heard of this and sent a boy of fifteen, Lachlan MacIntosh, to get through the cordon sealing off the town and warn the company at Moy. This he did and the Prince was roused from his seat before the fire, or from his bed — there are conflicting stories — to join his men encamped by Loch Moy.

The redoubtable 'Colonel Anne' as she was affectionately called, had, with commendable foresight, however, prepared against such an eventuality by sending four men under Donald Frazer, the Moy blacksmith, to keep a watch on Wade's road to Inverness. They waited in the woods by the roadside at Craig-an-Oin, and doubtless had some warning of the approach of Loudon's men in the dark.

It is not to the credit of Macleod that he who had once given expectation of his joining the Prince should now be leading a detachment of men into this furtive enterprise against him. But that was how it was. One can imagine the columns stealthily advancing in the dark then suddenly the woods leaping into gunfire and the battle cries of Locheil and Keppoch, now here, now there, 'advance Locheil!' They had walked into the Prince's army! Turn and flee for your lives! What a stumbling, shouting, pushing and confusion! Of those who fell in the mud, only one failed to rise again — alas, the piper of Macleod, a MacCrimmon. How many of that band, one wonders, had real stomach for the enterprise?

Thus did Frazer the blacksmith with four other brave fellows create the impression of a substantial ambush.

The Prince next day followed up the advantage of the strange 'Rout of Moy' by advancing on Inverness. Loudon did not want to receive him but left a garrison at the castle under Grant of Rothiemurchus, an ancestor of Elizabeth Grant who has left us such charming vignettes of dancing in Strathspey and of evenings with Niel Gow at the Inn at Inver. In Inverness, the Prince lodged with Lady MacIntosh's mother and held a ball. A month or so later, much to the old lady's discomfiture, Cumberland occupied the same room in her house and slept in the same bed as the Prince. She was reported to have said — and we can sympathize with her — 'I have had two King's bairns living with me in my time, and, to tell the truth, I wish I may never hae anither'.

Lady MacIntosh was a cousin of Lord George Murray, the redoubtable tactician and strategist who did so much for the Highland army in the face of the Prince's distrust. She is one of Scotland's great ladies of the eighteenth century.

The reel *Knit the Pocky* which Bremner published is entitled *Lady MacIntosh* by Stewart (*c*.1761). Thus there are two different reels named after the celebrated lady.

Duke of Hamilton's Reel

The title of Duke of Hamilton was first conferred, along with that of Marquis of Clydesdale, on James, Earl of Arran, elder son of the second Marquis of Hamilton. The dukedom passed to the Douglas family through the marriage of Anne, the successor of the Second Duke in the seventeenth century.

The Duke of Hamilton is hereditary keeper of Holyrood House and premier peer of Scotland.

The reel under consideration was first published along with the Country Dance bearing its name in Walsh's *Caledonian Country Dances* (*c.* 1754). The tune also appears in Bremner about the same time. The contemporary duke was the Sixth. He assumed the title in 1745 and died prematurely in 1758. He it was who fell in love with the youngest Miss Scott of Harden an excellent singer of the native songs and the reigning beauty of the time. He had her picture painted, but to everyone's surprise, the affair seemed to stop there. Next we find him turning to another, more celebrated beauty, an Irish one this time, Elizabeth Gunning, whom he married in 1752. Her two sons both succeeded to the title and after a period of widowhood she married the Duke of Argyll (see *Argyll's Bowling Green*), thus earning the name of 'The Double Duchess'. Two sons of this second marriage succeeded to the dukedom of Argyll. Here is something of a record.

Elizabeth Gunning's beauty was absolute. It owed nothing to the intelligence nor the personality. It was a perfection of form that has its own claim on immortality, and as one would expect, attracted the attention of more than one artist, as of more than one duke.

Checking through the eighteenth century dance music collections, I notice three reels which were probably written in her honour (*Riddell, Dow* and *Cumming*). Exactly which Duke of Hamilton is commemorated by the present reel, however, one cannot be sure.

Duke of Perth

The tune *Duke of Perth* or *The Duke of Perth's Reel* is first recorded in the Drummond Castle MS. (1734), where it is written as a rant. Scottish Country Dancers prefer it as a Scottish Measure.

The title 'Duke of Perth' was bestowed on James Drummond,

Fourth Earl of Perth, by the exiled King James in 1695. His eldest son was as resolute in the Jacobite cause as his father, strongly opposed the union with England in 1707 and joined in the rebellion in 1715. He died in Paris in 1730. The Duke of Perth who supported Prince Charlie in the '45 was the Third.

The 'Duke of Perth' giving his name to the reel was probably the First.

The dance of that name, published by the R.S.C.D.S., is taken from an early nineteenth century publication, although a version is contained in the Blantyre MS. (c. 1805). How the alternative titles arise — *Pease Strae*, a song of the countryside, and *Broun's Reel*, a tune first published in Stewart's *Collection* (c. 1761) — is not known. Possibly the same dance, or one very close to it, has been found associated with these tunes.

Dumbarton's Drums

> Dumbarton's drums beat bonnie, O,
> When they mind me of my dear Johnie, O;
>> How happy am I
>> When my soldier is by,
> While he kisses and blesses his Annie, O!
> 'Tis a soldier alone can delight me, O,
> For his graceful looks do invite me, O;
>> While guarded in his arms,
>> I'll fear no war's alarms,
> Neither danger nor death shall e'er fright me, O.

These words first reached the printed page in Allan Ramsay's *Tea Table Miscellany* (1723). It is easy to see how they could be identified with Dumbarton, the former capital of the Strathclyde kingdom of the Britons and now a busy county town overlooked by its impressive and lonely rock and castle.

However, it is altogether more probable that the Dumbarton of the song is the Earl of Dumbarton who was appointed by King James VII to the command of his forces in Scotland, and who defeated the insurrection — the 'Monmouth Rebellion' — led by the Earl of Argyll (cf. p.45), June 18, 1685. He was originally George Douglas, thid son of the Marquis of Douglas, who, after serving the King of France, was raised to his earldom by Charles II (1675). When James VII was deposed in favour of his daughter Mary and her husband William of Orange, Dumbarton retired to France with the King and died there in 1692. The title died with his son who, ironically, served the Hanoverian cause in 1715.

The tune *Dumbarton's Drums* is a jaunty Scottish Measure.

The Duran Ranger

This is a corruption of the name *Durham Ranger*, the name of a popular artificial fly used by salmon anglers. It was first devised by James Wright, a notable fly maker of Sprouston, near Kelso, on the occasion of the visit of a group of anglers from Durham to the local water, around 1865. The tune and the dance were collected in the Borders in the 1930's by Ian Jamieson of Galashiels, who collected the dances in the so-called *Border Book of Country Dances*.

The Dusty Miller

The Dusty Miller is an old song in 3/2 time, a class of tune known as the triple-time hornpipe. Like most tunes of this class, it can be modified into a 6/8 jig, and this is how it is used in the R.S.C.D.S. setting for this dance.

Here is a stanza and chorus of Burns' version of the traditional song:

> Hey the dusty miller
>   And his dusty coat;
> He will win a shilling
>   Or he spend a groat:
>
> Dusty was the coat,
>   Dusty was the colour,
> Dusty was the kiss
>   That I gat frae the miller.

But, of course, these words were not intended for the 6/8 version of the tune.

The Edinburgh Volunteers

This Country Dance was one of the favourite dances of the year 1796. The Edinburgh Volunteers formed in 1794 for local defence during the Napoleonic Wars, were an early version of what was known as the 'Home Guard' in the Second World War.

The initial corps numbered about 785. Their uniform was a blue coat, lapelled with black velvet, cut away from below the breast, with broad heavy square skirts, a row of buttons round the cuff, gold epaulettes for all ranks, white vest and breeches, with white cotton stockings, a round hat with a cockade and black feather on the left side. Two of the companies were grenadiers of unusual stature which gave them some celebrity.

The Volunteers were disbanded in 1802, but had to be re-formed when a new invasion threatened in the next year. At the height of the preparations, a beacon on Hume Castle was lighted in mistake or error, and soon the whole beacon warning system was in operation. The Volunteers were on the march to their several rendezvous all over Scotland and some in the Borders seized every horse available to hurry to their post in case they should be late, then turned them loose to find their own way home.

As Henry Cockburn tells us, events in France were on everyone's lips during these years. The unemployment and displacement of labour caused by the introduction of machinery on a large scale was producing severe social unrest at home. Every complaint against the Government or about lack of suffrage was regarded as seditious, and it would take a book in itself to discuss the pressures and events, the hunger and cruelty of industrial life in these times.

Yet men would defend their country, good or bad. 'Does haughty Gaul invasion threaten?' demanded Burns, while 'man's inhumanity to man' at home made 'countless thousands mourn'.

The Eight Men of Moidart

By the usual accounting, there were 'seven' men of Moidart — the confederates of Prince Charles Edward Stewart who accompanied him on his journey from France to Scotland to claim his own. They were: (1) William, Marquis of Tullibardine, the rightful Duke of Atholl who had lost his title in supporting the rebellion of 1715, (2) Sir John Macdonald, an Irish soldier of fortune, (3)

Angus Macdonald, brother of the Laird of Kinloch-moidart, (4) Sir Thomas Sheridan, the Prince's old tutor, (5) Col. Francis Strickland, a prominent Westmorland Jacobite and tutor to Charles, (6) Col. John William O'Sullivan, another Irish solder and (7) George Kelly, a hard-drinking Irishman.

A strangely unprepossessing group one would say. Nevertheless, these were the companions of the Prince when he set sail on June 21, 1745, in a chartered frigate, the *Doutelle*, of 44 guns, accompanied by an escort, the *Elizabeth*, of 68 guns and 700 men. The *Elizabeth* fell foul of an English man-o'-war, west of the Lizard, and after an engagement lasting several hours was obliged to return to port. The *Doutelle* escaped and reached the Outer Hebrides around July 23, 1745. Here, on the delightful isle of Eriskay, the Prince first set foot on Scottish soil, on the sandy beach henceforth known as Coilleag a' Phrionnsa (The Prince's Strand).

The Eightsome Reel

This, the most popular Scottish social dance (except perhaps for *Strip the Willow* and *The Gay Gordons*), combines features of the *Scotch Reel* and the *Quadrille*. It is not a Country Dance. Rather is it a square and round reel incorporating characteristics of the round reel of the West Highlands which survives to-day only in Cape Breton. Reels for four couples — or 'eightsomes' — are to be found in some manuscript collections dating from the early nineteenth century, but according to information given Miss Milligan the *Eightsome Reel* was devised by the Earl of Dunmore and several friends from their recollections of *Round Reels*, in the early 1870's, at the time of the Atholl Gathering Ball. Shortly thereafter, it was introduced to the Portree Ball, and to the Perth Hunt Ball. There is no disputing its subsequent popularity.

A version of this dance commonly enjoyed in the North-Eastern provinces of Scotland, and distinguished by the R.S.C.D.S. as the 'Buchan' *Eightsome* — from the district of Buchan — is preferred by many.

The Fairy Dance

The Fairy Dance is a very popular *Highland Reel* tune, properly called *The Largo Fairy Dance*, and was composed by Nathaniel Gow.

75

Fergus MacIvor or Waverley

This title alludes to an incident which occurred in the trial of some of the important Jacobites who were left to occupy Carlisle Castle and who thereby, inevitably and uselessly, were doomed to capture and execution. Sir Walter Scott describes it as follows in his first novel, *Waverley*:

> It was the third sitting of the court, and there were two men at the bar. The verdict of GUILTY was already pronounced. Edward just glanced at the bar during the momentous pause which ensued. There was no mistaking the stately form and noble features of Fergus Mac-Ivor, although his dress was squalid and his countenance tinged with the sickly yellow hue of long and close imprisonment. By his side was Evan Maccombich. Edward felt sick and dizzy as he gazed on them; but he was recalled to himself as the Clerk of the Arraigns pronounced the solemn words: 'Fergus Mac-Ivor of Glennaquoich, otherwise called Vich Ian Vohr, and Evan Mac-Ivor, in the Dhu of Tarrascleugh, otherwise called Evan Dhu, otherwise called Evan Maccombich, or Evan Dhu Maccombich — you, and each of you, stand attainted of high treason. What have you to say for yourselves why the Court should not pronounce judgment against you, that you die according to law?
>
> Fergus, as the presiding Judge was putting on the fatal cap of judgment, placed his own bonnet upon his head, regarded him with a steadfast and stern look, and replied in a firm voice, 'I cannot let this numerous audience suppose that to such an appeal I have no answer to make. But what I have to say, you would not bear to hear, for my defence would be your condemnation. Proceed, then, in the name of God, to do what is permitted to you. Yesterday, and the day before, you have condemned loyal and honourable blood to be poured forth like water. Spare not mine. Were that of all my ancestors in my veins, I would have peril'd it in this quarrel.' He resumed his seat.
>
> Evan Maccombich looked at him with great earnestness, and, rising up, seemed anxious to speak; but the confusion of the court, and the perplexity arising from thinking in a language different from that in which he was to express himself, kept him silent. There was a murmur of compassion among the spectators, from an idea that the poor fellow intended to plead the influence of his superior as an excuse for his crime. The Judge commanded silence, and encouraged Evan to proceed.
>
> 'I was only ganging to say, my Lord,' said Evan, in what he meant to be in an insinuating manner, 'that if your excellent honour, and the honourable Court, would let Vich Ian Vohr go free just this once, and let him gae back to France, and not to trouble King George's government again, that ony six o' the very best of his clan

76

will be willing to be justified in his stead; and if you'll just let me gae down to Glannaquoich, I'll fetch them up to ye mysel' to head or hang, and you may begin wi' me the very first man.'

Notwithstanding the solemnity of the occasion, a sort of laugh was heard in the court at the extraordinary nature of the proposal. The Judge checked this indecency, and Evan, looking sternly around, when the murmur abated, 'If the Saxon gentlemen are laughing,' he said, 'because a poor man, such as me, thinks my life, or the life of six of my degree, is worth that of Vich Ian Vohr, it's like enough they may be right; but if they laugh because they think I would not keep my word, and come back to redeem him, I can tell them they ken neither the heart of a Hielandman nor the honour of a gentleman.'

There was no further inclination to laugh among the audience, and a dead silence ensued.

The Judge then pronounced upon both prisoners the sentence of the law of high treason, with all its horrible accompaniments. The execution was appointed for the ensuing day. 'For you, Fergus Mac-Ivor,' continued the Judge, 'I can hold no hope of mercy. You must prepare against to-morrow for your last sufferings here, and your great audit hereafter.'

'I desire nothing else, my lord,' answered Fergus, in the same manly and firm tone.

The hard eyes of Evan, which had been perpetually bent on his Chief, were moistened with a tear. 'For you, poor ignorant man,' continued the Judge, 'who, following the ideas in which you have been educated, have this day given us a striking example how the loyalty due to the king and state alone, is, from your unhappy idea of clanship, transferred to some ambitious individual, I say, I feel so much compassion, that if you can make up your mind to petition for grace, I will endeavour to procure it for you. Otherwise . . .'

'Grace me no grace,' said Evan, 'since you are to shed Vich Ian Vohr's blood, the only favour I would accept from you is — to bid them loose my hands and gie me my claymore, and bide you just a minute sitting where you are!'

'Remove the prisoners,' said the Judge; 'his blood be upon his own head!'

The Flowers of Edinburgh

This tune first appears in 1742, with the title *My love's bonny when she smiles on me*, then reappears in 1751 with its present title. It is of the category of a Scottish Measure. Burns regarded it as 'one of the many effusions of Jacobitism', and that since the words of the song then current were in no way connected with the title, presumed that there had existed a more relevant set of words. The change of title certainly occurs at a very suspicious time.

The Foula Reel

This, once better known in Shetland as the *Shalds o' Foula*, is a weaving folk dance of which *Strip the Willow* and *The Hebridean Weaving Lilt* (collected by the late Mrs. MacNab and published by the R.S.C.D.S.) are also examples. In these the movements and figures simulate the operations of weaving. The most comprehensive surviving dance of this kind is the Swedish *Vava Vadmal* and clearly it is a class of dance found in the parts of Scotland in which Norse influence or occupation has occurred. *Foula* or 'fowl island' is a neighbour of the Shetlands, famous for its woollens.

Foursome Reel

The *Foursome Reel* is the ballroom version of the traditional 'linear' reel or *'Highland'* or *'Scotch' Reel*. It is the reel-of-four executed in Strathspey and Athol styles in sequence, a 'medley' indeed, but not a Country Dance. There was no more universally enjoyed dance in the ballrooms of Europe at one time.

The Fyket

The 'fyket' — the 'fidgety'. To 'fyke' means to fidget or be restlessly fussy. A punctilious or fastidious person is 'fikey', and he who has no time to worry over such 'fikery' shall not make a 'fyke' (fuss) about it.

A reel of this name appears in Bremner's first collection and also in Part Third of Gow's *Complete Repository*, where it is marked 'very old'. It was included as a Strathspey in the fifth Gow *Collection* or, at any rate, as a Strathspey based on the reel.

The R.S.C.D.S. use a jig of the same name which appears to be a free variation of the reel in jig rhythm, of which the Society does not acknowledge the source. The dance figures are derived from the Blantyre MS. (*c.* 1805).

The Gates of Edinburgh

The 'gates' of Edinburgh are, of course, the 'streets' — particularly Canongate and Cowgate, still so called, and the Highgate now called High Street. The word 'gate' being the Germanic for 'street' or 'way' and generally used in the burghs of Scotland and to a varying extent in those of Eastern England, especially Northumberland.

The change from 'gate' to 'street' took place in Victorian times, particularly in Glasgow where commerce and industrial growth transfigured the lovely old town. Surprisingly enough, 'the' Gallowgate and 'the' Drygate survived while the Stockwell, Bridge and High 'gates', conformed to the new fashion. In Edinburgh, the Canongate and Cowgate were indestructible as names, but the great new street of the new town was called Prince's *Street*.

Other names for the 'rues' of the 'toun' were *wynd* and *raw* (row). A *wynd* was a narrow street bounded by tenements and a *raw* was a row or terrace of houses. If a street took a bend, that portion would be called a 'bow' and in Edinburgh we have one of the most distinguished of these, identified along its length as 'west', 'upper', 'nether' and 'foot'.

The topography of old Edinburgh was irregular; the castle rock swept down into ravines or cuts and the city clustered round the rock, its 'gates' following the violent contours with dramatic and picturesque effect.

The Gentle Shepherd

This was the title of a celebrated pastoral in Scots verse by Allan Ramsay, the Edinburgh bookseller and poet, published in 1725. The setting of the play is the undulating Midlothian countryside around the village of Penicuik.

'Let Glasgow Flourish' is the armorial motto of the Glasgow coat of arms. It is an abbreviation of 'Lord, let Glasgow flourish through the preaching of thy word and praising thy Name' which was inscribed round the arms of the city in the early seventeenth century. It was not until the nineteenth century, however, that steps were taken to have the City Arms authorized by Lord Lyon, King-of-Arms, and this was done in October 1866.

Glasgow Flourish

Some of the details of the Glasgow 'Toune Armes' may be of interest. Their heraldic motifs — oak tree, bird, fish and bell — appear in the seals of the early bishops of Glasgow and certainly in the burgh arms by the sixteenth century. To discover the significance of these motifs, it is necessary to go back to St. Kentigern, commonly known as St. Mungo, who founded a church or monastery in the sixteenth century on the site now occupied by the cathedral. St. Mungo knew this site as one of a number of pleasant eminences, pastoral and serene, sloping down to the river on the south side, and to the east a gentle ravine or glen through which chattered the Molendinar burn — now conducted to the Clyde by means of an unfeeling conduit or sewer. One day, the legend goes, the Queen of Cadzow applied to St. Mungo to help her find a ring, a token from her husband King Roderick, which she had lost and which her jealous husband suspected her of having given to a lover. The Saint, doubtless moved by the vehemence of the lady's petition, sent one of his followers to catch a fish in

80

the river and bring it to him. This was done and behold, what did the fish hold in its mouth but the lost ring, and thus was the lady rescued from an unhappy fate.

Then St. Serf of Culross ('Cu'ross') in Fife had a pet robin which was accidentally killed by his disciples, and brought to life again by St. Mungo. Perhaps it was on the same visit that one night the lamps of the monastery at Culross went out. St. Mungo, however, nothing daunted, tore a frozen bough from a tree and set it alight by making the Sign of the Cross over it. Hence the tree and the bird in the emblem of Glasgow.

The bell in the emblem represents a bell brought from Rome by the worthy patron, and which, we are told, was used as the town 'dead' bell up to the Reformation. So, true to her begettors, Glasgow flourishes to-day with the mementoes of her legends, familiar devices on the seals of her medieval prelates, emblazoned on the sides of her buses and on all her official property.

It is difficult to imagine the City of Glasgow to-day as the spacious, elegant, tranquil city of which so many English travellers rhapsodied in the seventeenth and eighteenth centuries — 'a place of great extent and good situation', (Morer, *Short account of Scotland*, 1689) its four principal streets which Defoe thought (1727) the 'fairest for breadth, and the finest built' that he had ever seen 'in one city together'.

Visitors to-day often remark the marked difference in tempo, *joie de vivre*, between Glasgow and Edinburgh. The one, close to the sea routes to the Highlands and the Americas, a commercial and industrial centre, a Celtic city; the other, reserved, more beautiful now in a romantic way, the royal seat, the tall buildings of the medieval town an extention of those across the North Sea.

The tune *Glasgow Flourish* was first published in Joshua Campbell's *Collection*, along with such reels as *Glasgow Bells*, *Glasgow College* and *Glasgow Ladys*, all probably of his own composition. Joshua, a cooper, led the band at the Glasgow dance assemblies in his day (late eighteenth century) and was appointed to the office of player of the Tolbooth bells in 1772. For a comparative view of Edinburgh and Glasgow at this period it is interesting to turn to 'Senex', the chronicler of the Glasgow of his time, who leaves us an account of a youthful visit to the capital in the summer of 1784.

'Mr. Ferrier and his Daughters having spent eight days with us, resolved to return to Edinburgh by the Edinburgh Diligence, which

81

was a Chaise and Pair. It set off daily from the Saracen's Head Inn in the Gallowgate, at 7 o'clock in the morning, and arrived in Edinburgh at 8 o'clock at night, I think the price of the Seat was 7s. 6d.; but I am not sure of this, as I did not pay for my Seat, Mr. Ferrier having engaged the whole Vehicle. I slept very little the night before my departure, thinking on the grand sights that I was to see in Edinburgh, and was up next morning when the Ramshorn Bell was ringing 6 o'clock. All our Luggage being ready, and a Farewell given to our fireside relatives and friends, the Minister, his Daughters, and myself set out on foot for the Saracen's Head Inn, by way of the Gallowgate. As we passed along that Street we came to the Quarters of Gabriel Watson, who was then unloading the great Newcastle Waggon. This was a ponderous Machine, with 6 broad wheels, and drawn by 8 horses. It generally carried a great portion of the Glasgow Linen and Cotton Manufactures to the London Market. It travelled at the rate of 25 miles per day, and was 3 weeks upon the road between Glasgow and London, resting always upon the Sundays. It was said that the first Trip which Mr. John M'Illquhan made to London was in this Conveyance. I remember of my Father mentioning that he went for the first time to London in the year 1749. He sailed from Borrowstownness on board of a Trading Vessel, which at that time was considered the best mode of Conveyance from Glasgow to the English Capital. What is curious, there being then in Glasgow another Gentleman of the same Christian and Surname as my Father, our Citizens, after my Father's return from London, distinguished him from his namesake by calling my Father 'London John'. So remarkable was a sight of London at that time considered in Glasgow.

After passing Gabriel Watson's Quarters in the Gallowgate, we soon arrived in sight of the noted Sign of the Saracen's Head, and truly a frightful Fellow he was; with his truculent countenance, and glaring eyes, his hooked Scimitar and Crimson Eastern dress, he was indeed the very Image of the Ghoul in the Arabian Nights. It is singular how this Sign should have come down to our own times. We still see the Signs of the Saracen's Head and of the Turk's Head, thus showing the lingering reminiscences of the Crusades, during which time a Turk was looked upon with horror, as a sort of relentless demon. Having arrived at the Saracen's Head Inn, a few minutes before 7 o'clock in the morning, we waited a short time until the horses were put to the Diligence.

This celebrated Inn is still to the fore, but converted into Shops and small Dwelling Houses. The great Hall in which our Civic Rulers and our County Gentlemen were wont to hold their feasts, and where our Glasgow Belles 'tripped it on the light fantastic toe', is now turned into a Reading-School (1856). It still shows the remains of an elegant and commodious Place of Assembly, and quite worthy of the times in which it was erected.

The Horses being now harnessed, and our Luggage strapped and secured on the top of the Diligence, we fairly set off for the great Town of Edinburgh. 'Coachy', however, did not show much diligence in the use of his Whip, for we travelled very slowly — not more, perhaps, than 6 miles in the hour — and whenever any little Eminence occurred, the Horses were allowed to take a comfortable walk to its summit. We arrived at Cumbernauld shortly after 9 o'clock, where we stopped upwards of an hour and a half, in order to give us time for Breakfast, and to allow a little rest and a feed to our Horses, they being destined to carry us forward another Stage.

After a comfortable Dejeuner, we again took our places in the Diligence, and set out upon our journey at the former canny Pace. About 2 o'clock we arrived at the famous and ancient Town of Linlithgow, where we stopped (as at last Stage) fully an hour and a half, which gave us plenty of time, not only to Dine, but also to take a walk over the Town, and to see all the Curiosities of the Place; amongst these I felt most interest in examining the celebrated 'Lithgo' Wells'. The Edinburgh Folks used to laugh at Glasgow vulgarity, but in those days we paid them back in their own coin; and I believe that we had the best of it, as the following notable Distich of the times can verify:

Lithgo' for Wells,
Glasgow for Bells,
Falkirk for Beeves (Falkirk for Beans and Pease),
Edinburgh for Whores and Thieves.

After a very comfortable Dinner at Linlithgow, we again took our Seats in the Diligence, expecting to get a little quicker forward, seeing that the Horses were now changed; but in this we were disappointed, for we just proceeded at the former jog-trot pace for a couple of hours or so, when we stopped at an Inn upon the Road, where the Horses were fed and got a long rest, to enable them to finish the remaining Stage of our Journey. In the meantime, while the Horses were thus resting and feeding, we had our Tea, and spent the time in the best manner we could, but rather tired at the delay. Being again Seated as before, we drove on, and were finally set down safely in the Grass Market of Edinburgh about 8 o'clock at night.

About this time there was a class of men in Edinburgh called 'Caddies', who received Licenses from the Magistrates to act as Porters. The Caddies bore a high character for honesty and good conduct, so much so, that they were frequently entrusted with the charge of delivering large Sums of Money, and of very valuable Articles; and almost in no instance had any of them been found guilty of committing the slightest breach of trust. It was to one of these Caddies that Mr. Ferrier delivered our Luggage, with directions where to take it. In the meantime, we proceeded from the Grass Market up the West Bow to the Lawn Market, where Mr. Ferrier had his residence. His House was near the Lucken Booths, on the North side of the Lawn Market, and up two stairs; the passage to it rather dark and narrow. It was an old-fashioned House, and did not appear to me to possess much grandeur. The Shopkeepers in the Lawn Market very generally had portions of their Goods exposed upon the Footpath of the Street, on the outside of their Shop Doors; this was especially the case with Vendors of coarse Linens and Woollens.

St. Giles' Church was then disfigured by the Lucken Booths, and by a narrow Lane called the Creams, both of which have been removed. The South Bridge, now so prominent to the view of Strangers, was not in existence at the period in question, so that this part of Edinburgh had then a very different appearance from what it has at present. The Tron Church was surrounded by old Buildings, with narrow closes running southwards to the Cowgate, and Niddry's Wynd, Merlin's Wynd, and Kennedy's Close being then to the fore. Of course, Adam's Square had not yet been built.

The Exchange at this time was quite neglected by the Edinburgh Merchants, who met in the High Street, where the old Cross of Edinburgh once stood, and where their Forefathers met in olden times: just as our neighbouring Farmers prefer to meet at the Head of the Stockwell, because that Place was once our Cattle Market.

The custom of throwing out Nuisances of all kind from the Windows of Houses in the Old Town, after 10 o'clock at night, was then in full vigour, and the celebrated cry of 'gardez-vous' (changed to 'gardiloo') was still heard in the narrow Lanes and Closes of 'Auld Reekie'. In fact, there were no common Sewers whatever at that time in the Old Town, and the principal Streets and Wynds being situated upon a Hill, the natural descent to the lower Grounds formed a cheap and easy Drain for carrying off the contaminated domestic Streams. The Old Town Guard House, of ancient celebrity, and the Weigh House, which were situated at the Lucken Booths, near the Lawn Market, were at this time in existence, but have since been pulled down. The Edinburgh University was a clump of mean old Buildings, situated among dirty Streets, and possessing none of those immense stone Pillars which now grace its front to Nicholson Street. I remember at a later period that it was deemed extremely dangerous to convey these massy Columns across the Bridges, lest their immense weight should break down the said Bridges. I think they were about 30 feet in height, and each consisted of a single Stone. The High School of Edinburgh was, at the time of my visit, situated at a short distance from the present Royal Infirmary, but I have not a distinct recollection what like it was, only that it was two Stories in height. The Register Office was in the process of building, but not above one-third of the present Erection at that time existed, and the Records were not yet deposited there. The Surgeons' Hall, at the period in question, stood about 300 feet from the Royal Infirmary, and was rather a neat building. All the Banks were situated in narrow, and generally in dark, Closes of the Old Town. The Earthen Mound was a shapeless mass, not one half of its present height, and scarcely passable for glaur and nastiness.

The North Loch (or, the Nor-Loch, as it was more generally called) was still a mere Swamp, with no proper drainage, and full of Springs, at the same time receiving the fulzie of the houses on the north side of the Castlehill, Lawn Market, Lucken Booths, and High Street. The Park called the Meadows, though frequented as a walk in Summer, was in a most abominable state in Winter, owing to the putrid exhalations from stagnant water to it from Bristo Street, Potter Row, George's Square, Laurieston, Goosedubbs, and Sciennes. As for the New Town, — Prince's Street and George's Street were pretty well built upon, but the Cross Streets, such as St. David Street, Hanover Street, and Frederick Street, were but partially filled up with Buildings; Castle Street and Charlotte Street were merely laid off for Feuing. St. James's Square was still unfinished at this period, though partially built, a considerable delay having taken place with regard to completing the Titles to the piece of Ground constituting this Square.

The Glasgow Highlanders

The dance, *Glasgow Highlanders*, is a product of the late nineteenth century, incorporating characteristics of the Country Dance and the Strathspey Reel in a most effective and successful way. The tune of that name, inseparably associated with the dance, is of the character of an Irish hornpipe. The composer of the dance and/or tune is unknown, which is a pity.

The growth of Glasgow in the nineteenth century drew thousands of Highlanders into its vortex. Highland or Gaelic Societies or Clubs had already sprung into being in that city (1780) and also in Edinburgh (1783) and Aberdeen (*c.* 1820), bringing the displaced 'sons of Ossian', as they often liked to style themselves, into fellowship and social contact. By the end of the nineteenth century, there was no doubt that the 'London Scottish' and the 'Glasgow Highlanders' were the most numerous and active of the city Gaels, as indeed they remain to this day.

The Golden Pheasant

This is the name of a pheasant introduced to the estates of Atholl some time around 1870. It was not indigenous to Scotland.

Green Grow the Rashes

Here is a really old tune. It appears as *The Grant's Rant* in Bremner's *Reels* 1759; but it was long the vehicle of a gay old song which was still well known in Burns' day. The germ of the air appears in the Straloch MS. 1627, under the title of *A dance: Green Grow the Rashes*, and a song of a similar name *Cou thou me the raschyes green* is listed in that valuable old Scots book *The Complaynt* (*c.* 1549).

Burns turned his inspired hand to the lyric and it has the distinction of being the first which he contributed to the *Musical Museum* (1787) No. 77. He also amused himself in adding to the store of coarser lines associated with the tune but these are of no moment.

Green grow the rashes, O
Green grow the rashes, O,
The sweetest hours that e'er I spent,
Were spent amang the lasses, O.
Auld nature swears the lovely dears
Her noblest works she classes, O;
Her 'prentice hand she tried on man,
And then she made the lasses, O.

Hamilton House

Hamilton House was the rather splendid palace of the Dukes of Hamilton situated in the pleasant town of that name, not far from Glasgow. After many rebuildings and extensions throughout the years, what was originally but a small rectangular tower in 1591, grew into 'one of the most magnificent structures in Great Britain' by the early nineteenth century. The art treasures embowered here were of great renown, particularly Rubens' *Daniel in the Lion's Den*, which was generally considered by distinguished travellers in the late eighteenth century as worthy of a visit on its own.

In these days tourism was the prerogative of the privileged few, becoming something of a fashion, and it was customary for travellers of social standing to be permitted to view the art treasures and antiquities in certain noble houses. Hamilton House was one of these, and one of the attractions of the beautiful upper reaches of the Clyde.

One distinguished visitor who unfortunately was turned away from Hamilton House, was William Wordsworth when, along with Coleridge and his sister Dorothy, he called there in 1803. The Duke himself was not in residence at the time and his servants obviously decided that the Wordsworths did not warrant the privilege of viewing the famous picture gallery, which was a pity.

The tune *Hamilton House* is a jig; the dance is first noted in the late eighteenth century and the great house it commemorates was literally undermined, sitting, as it did, on top of a rich coal field.

87

Haughs o' Cromdale

Although the dance presented under this name by the R.S.C.-D.S. was collected in the Borders, Cromdale ('Crooked Dale') is a district in Strathspey. The tune was first published by Oswald under the name: *Wat ye how the Play began?* in his Pocket Companion *c.* 1740; but it appears as *The Haws of Cromdale*, a ballad, in Johnson's *Musical Museum*, beginning with the line 'As I came in by Achindown'.

The word 'Haugh (pronounced 'haw', or 'hoch' as in 'loch') for river meadow, is common in the Scottish Lowlands and one suspects that it would be of Anglian origin; but it is more likely to be Celtic (esp. Brithonic), related to the word *halech*.

The ballad described an event which took place during the Civil War when some Royalist Highlanders were routed by a detachment of the 'Army of the Covenant' on the 'Haughs o' Cromdale' only to be avenged by the great Montrose shortly thereafter.

Haymakers

The *Haymakers* was a most popular dance in the late eighteenth century and gained entrée long before Country Dances to many of the social gatherings in the Highlands. It was, of course, none other than the English *Sir Roger de Coverley* and what became known as the *Virginia Reel* in New England. The tune, known in Scotland as *The Mautman (Maltman) comes on Monday*, is a 9/8 jig and hence the normal Scottish technique is not suitable. A running step is requisite.

Highland Laddie

The R.S.C.D.S. Country Dance of this name is taken from Walsh's *Caledonian Country Dances* (1754), where it is set to the tune of the old song of that name. The tune, an excellent Scottish Measure, is well known, and has existed in several different setts germinating from an original strain which is very old. Verses to the tunes are similarly various, mostly of a Jacobite slant; Ramsay and Burns both had a go at it. Here is a verse of Burns':

88

The bonniest lad that e'er I saw,
  Bonnie laddie, Highland laddie,
Wore a plaid and was fu' braw,
  Bonnie laddie, Highland laddie.
On his head a bonnet blue,
  Bonnie laddie, Highland laddie,
His royal heart was firm and true,
  Bonnie laddie, Highland laddie.

Parodies of the ditty were easily developed:

Where hae ye been a' day,
  Bonnie laddie, Highland laddie,
Doun the back o' Bell's brae,
  Courtin' Maggie, courtin' Maggie.

Another sett of the air was given verses by Burns — 'As I came o'er the Cairney Mount' — and this is the principal tune set to the Country Dance by the R.S.C.D.S.

As I came o'er the Cairney mount,
  And down amang the blooming heather,
Kindly stood the milking shiel,
  To shelter frae the stormy weather.

O my bonnie Highland lad,
  My winsome, weel far'd Highland laddie;
Wha wad mind the wind and rain,
  Sae weel row'd in his tartan plaidie.

The Highland Reel

The dance called *The Highland Reel* in the R.S.C.D.S. collection is not what was generally known as the *Highland Reel*, or *'Scotch' Reel*. It is a round-the-room variation of that dance, after the style of the *Dashing White Sergeant* and the Swedish Country Dances. It involves the 'set and reel' sequence of the *Highland Reel*, but the progression round the room, etc., is a nineteenth century elaboration.

I'll Gang Nae Mair to Yon Toun

One verse only of the old song has been recorded:

> I'll gang nae mair to yon toun,
>> O, never a' my life again;
> I'll ne'er gae back to yon toun
>> To seek anither wife again.

The tune appears in several eighteenth century collections and was observed to be a great favourite of George IV during his visit to Edinburgh in 1822.

Burns wrote a happy effusion to this tune, in honour of his Jean:

> I'll aye ca' in by yon toun,
>> And by yon garden green again;
> I'll aye ca' in by yon toun,
>> And see my bonnie Jean again.

> There's nane shall ken, there's nane shall guess,
>> What brings me back the gate again,
> But she, my fairest faithfu' lass;
>> And stowlins we shall meet again.

However, Burns wrote another song to the tune, which testifies to his liking for it. He wished it played slowly for his purpose, however, and took the set of the tune in Bowie's *Collection*. This song is of special interest to lovers of Scottish dance and dance music because although it was initially written for Jean, Burns altered the name to 'Lucy' in honour of Lucy Johnston who married R.A. Oswald of Auchencruive, Ayrshire. Lucy was an ornament to the Edinburgh dancing assemblies of her time, a composer of reels and Strathspeys, and the dedicatee of tunes composed by the Gows and others. She was sadly lamented when she died of tuberculosis at the age of thirty in 1798.

> O, wat ye wha's in yon toun,
>> Ye see the e'ening sun upon?
> The fairest maid's in yon toun,
>> That e'ening sun is shining on.

> Now haply down yon gay green shaw,
>> She wanders by yon spreading tree;
> How blest ye flow'rs, that round her blaw
>> Ye catch the glances o' her e'e.

90

Stabilini, who led the orchestra at the concerts in St. Cecilia's Hall in Edinburgh during this period, introduced this tune as a *rondo* in a violin concerto he composed.

Inch of Perth

The word 'Inch' is derived from the Celtic word for island; *innis* in Gaelic and *ynys* in Welsh. The 'Inch' of Perth is a meadow which has been islanded by the river. The river, in this case, being the Tay. The town of Perth, once known as St. John's Toun (St. Johnstone), well deserves its pseudonym 'The Fair City', nestling as it does beside the crystal river, one of the best of the remaining salmon rivers of Scotland, where it follows the long gentle curves of its broad basin. The crags and slopes of Kinnoul Hill — the location of the performance of the mystic rites of Beltane, from time immemorial — drop close to the water and are linked to the town by a long bridge which has been much admired. On a clear day, especially, this is a noble sight.

The Inch of Perth is town property and now provides delightful grass sward for recreation. It has seen clan battles and great musters. It was here that Prince Charlie's army re-grouped and prepared for its march on the capital, although its reception from the burgesses of this historic town, so conspicuously involved with the spirit of the Reformation, was understandably subdued.

Near Perth, it should be remembered, lies Scone ('Skoon'), seat of the Pictish kings and of the early kings of united Scotland. It was here all Scotland's monarchs were crowned, Charles II being the last.

91

The Infare

The 'Infare' is the festive reception of the bride at her home-coming. The Infare-cake was broken over her head as she crossed the threshold of her new home. The tune to this dance is the old reel first printed in Bremner's *Collection* (1764), entitled *Will ye go and marry, Kettie?* Burns set words to it for inclusion in the *Museum* of which the following is the first verse:

> Will ye go and marry Katie,
> Can ye think tae tak a man.
> It's a pity ane sae pretty
> Should na do the thing they can.
> You a charming lovely creature,
> Wharfore wad ye lie y'er lane!
> Beauty's of a fading nature,
> Has a season and is gane.

The breaking of the Infare-cake was a widespread custom found in England as well as Scotland although there were some local variations in procedure. The symbolical association of the cake with fertility is a remnant of the pre-Christian religion or superstition of the Celtic tribes of Britain, and appears also in rites associated with Beltane, the Celtic counterpart to May Day. Fragments of the broken cake were distributed among the bystanders, and this was acknowledged to have the property of conjuring dreams of one's future wedding partner, if placed under one's pillow.

Invercauld's Reel

Invercauld's Reel is a beautiful tune, a good example of the Strathspey dance air at its best. The author is unknown, but the tune is in the Drummond Castle MS. (1734) and was published in several of the late eighteenth century collections.

Burns set one of his very earliest songs to this tune. He was but seventeen years of age when his pride was hurt by the disinterest, if not disdain, of the daughter of an adjacent farmer.

O Tibbie, I hae seen the day,
  Ye wadna been sae shy;
For laik o' gear ye lightly me,
  But, trowth, I care na by.

Yestreen I met you on the moor,
  Ye spak na but gaed by like stoure:
Ye geck at me because I'm poor,
  But fient a hair care I.

Invercauld is a village in the Braemar district of Aberdeenshire. The laird, Farquharson of Invercauld, is chief of that sept of Clan Chattan.

Jenny! Come down to Jock

Jock and Jenny are the perennial wooers of Scottish verse. 'Jock' for John, and 'Jenny' for Janet. So we have *The Wooing of Jock and Jenny; Jockey fou, Jenny fain* and many others.

The particular jig tune here concerned is doubtless much older than the particular verses which were best known in the eighteenth century beginning.

Jock he came here to woo,
  On ae feast day when he was fou;
And Jenny put on her best array,
  When she heard that Jocky was come that way.

Jenny she gaed up the stair,
  Sae privily to change her smock;
And aye sae loud her mother did rair,
  Hey, *Jenny*, come down to *Jock*!

the germ of which is believed by some to be *Rob's Jock* which is inserted in the sixteenth century Bannatyne MS.

Jenny Dang the Weaver or *Musselburgh*

'Dang' means to strike or beat. It could be used in the sense of 'getting the better of' and one suspects that the original song, which appears now to be lost, told a story in this tenor. A song collected by Herd in the eighteenth century, beginning 'As I cam in by Fisherrow', was sung to the reel tune *Jenny dang the weaver*. It is from this that its alternative title *Musselburgh* is derived:

93

As I cam in by Fisherrow,
Musselburgh was near me,
I threw off my mussel pock,
And courted wi' my deary.

O had her apron bidden down,
The Kirk wad ne'er hae kend it;
But since the word's gane thro' the town,
My dear I canna mend it.

But ye maun mount the cutty stool,
And I maun mount the pillar;
And that's the way the poor folks do,
Because they hae nae siller.

Up stairs, down stairs,
Timber stairs fears me.
I thought it lang to ly my lane,
When I'm sae near my dearie.

It is possible that this is a variant of the original song. Ramsay used the tune for a humerous poem of his own beginning 'O mither dear! I 'gin to fear', in which he uses the second and last verses of the above with slight modifications to suit the different circumstances — the confession of the young lady that her resistance to 'Johny' is fast declining and her mother's advice to 'get Johny's hand in holy band'.

Up stairs, down stairs
Timber stairs fear me;
I'm laith to ly a' night my lane,
And Johny's bed sae near me.

So goes Ramsay's chorus.

James Boswell's son, Sir Alexander Boswell, Bart., of Auchinleck, wrote an excellent set of verses for the tune, which one could imagine being closer to the original than those above as the following extracts may indicate:

Willie's wedding on the green,
The lassies bonnie witches,
Were a' dress'd out in aprons clean,
And braw white Sunday mutches:
Auld Maggie bade the lads tak' tent,
But Jock would not believe her;
But soon the fool his folly kent,
For Jenny dang the weaver.
   And Jenny dang, Jenny dang,
   Jenny dang the weaver;
   But soon the fool his folly kent,
   For Jenny dang the weaver.

At ilka country dance or reel,
Wi her he wad be bobbin';
When she sat down — he sat down.
And to her wad be gabbin';
Where'er she gaed, baith butt and ben,
The coof wad never leave her;
Aye kecklin' like a clockin' hen,
But Jenny dang the weaver.
   And Jenny dang, Jenny dang,
   Jenny dang the weaver;
   Aye kecklin' like a clockin' hen,
   But Jenny dang the weaver.

Hugh Paton, in his *Contemporaries of Burns*, recounts the tale that the tune *Jenny Dang the Weaver* was composed by the Rev. Mr. Gardner, minister of the parish of Birse, Aberdeenshire, an enthusiastic fiddler, on witnessing an incident in which his wife, Jenny, had occasion to strike at Jock the 'minister's man' — 'an idle sort of weaver' — for impudently refusing to clean the dirt off the minister's shoes. Whatever the relevance of this story, it is quoted as having occurred in the year 1746, a good twenty years after the tune was used by Ramsay, as we have seen.

> And a' that e'er my Jenny had,
> My Jenny had, my Jenny had,
> And a' that e'er my Jenny had,
>   Was ae bawbee.
>
> There's your plack and my plack,
> And your plack and my plack,
> And my plack and your plack,
>   And Jenny's bawbee.
>
> We'll put it in the pint stoup,
> The pint stoup, the pint stoup,
> We'll put it in the pint stoup,
>   And birl't a' three.

These are the verses which Herd collected.

The 'Bawbee' was equal in value to the halfpenny sterling. The 'plack', one farthing sterling. The 'stoup' is the tankard; and to 'birl't a' three' means to 'birl' or 'whirl' all three coins in the stoup.

The tune *Jenny's Bawbee* was a popular reel, and Sir Alex Boswell and one or two others turned their hand to producing new sets of verses. One of the versions required the tune to be played *andante* with good effect.

Perhaps a note on the names and relative values of the old Scottish coins will be appropriate here:

> Dyot = 1 penny Scots
> Boddle = 2 penny Scots
> Groat or Plack = 4 penny Scots
> Bawbee = 6 penny Scots
> Shilling = 12 penny Scots
> Merk = 13s. 4d. Scots
> Scots Pound = 20s. Scots.

The Scots pound was one-twelfth the value of the English or Sterling pound. English currency was adopted after the union in 1707 and the Scottish silver withdrawn. The copper coins continued in circulation for some years thereafter and kirk sessions complained of 'the dyots and other money that is not current' which they found in the collection boxes.

The Jimp Waist

'Jimp' here means 'slender' or 'neat'.

John o' Groat's House (Johnny Groat's House)

In the late fifteenth century, the family of Groat of Dutch or Flemish origin, obtained land in the district of Duncansby in the northernmost tip of Scotland. John de Groat was very probably sent by the King, as tradition has it, to take charge of the ferry which plied twelve miles across the dangerous currents of the Pentland Firth to Orkney. This ferry, indeed, appears at one time to have belonged to the Crown.

It is not really known which John o' Groat built the house or inn referred to by some travellers in the seventeenth century as the most northerly house in Scotland. The Rev. John Brand visited John o' Groat's and stayed overnight in the famous house in 1698. He tells us that the landing place was called 'John Grot's House, the northernmost house in Scotland; the man who now liveth in it and keepeth an inn there is called John Grot, who saith this house hath been in the possession of his predecessors of that name for some hundreds of years; which name of Grot is frequent in Caithness. Upon the sand of John Grot's house are found many small pleasant buckies and shells, beautified with diverse colours, which some use to put upon a string as beads, and account much of for their rarity. It is also observed of these shells that not one can be found altogether like another, and upon the review of the parcel I had I discovered some difference among them, which variety renders them the more beautiful.' (*Pinkerton's Voyages*, pp. iii, 801).

The house is no longer in existence; but it was, from all accounts, octagonal in shape, or at least the original structure was. The story goes that when the first John was advanced in years, disputes arose at the annual family gathering held on the anniversary of the Groat's arrival in Caithness, on the subject of precedence at table. There were eight claimants to the top place — the place by the door. So John built a house or chamber with eight doors and eight windows within which he placed a table of the same shape, thus enabling all to sit in 'top' place. In this odd way, harmony was restored.

This tradition is first recorded in the *Old Statistical Account of Canisbay* (late eighteenth century) but, strangely enough, is not referred to by any of the early travellers who left journals of their tours, including Pennant, the celebrated antiquarian.

Johnny McGill

John McGill was a celebrated itinerant dancing master and fiddler of Girvan, Ayrshire. The jig named after him is said to have been of his own composition.

Burns immortalized the tune with the words of his song *Tibbie Dunbar*. Another song, however, written by one Hector Macneill, entitled *Come under my Plaidy*, was also set to this tune. Both songs are included in Johnson's *Museum*.

Tibbie Dunbar
O, wilt thou go wi' me, sweet Tibbie Dunbar?
O, wilt thou go wi' me, sweet Tibbie Dunbar?
Wilt thou ride on a horse, or be drawn in a car,
Or walk by my side, O sweet Tibbie Dunbar?
I ken na thy daddie, his lands and his money;
I care na thy kin, sae high and sae lordly:
But say that thou'lt hae me for better or waur,
And come in thy coatie, sweet Tibbie Dunbar.

. . . .

Come under my Plaidy
Come under my plaidy, the night's ga'en to fa';
Come in frae the cauld blast, the drift and the snaw;
Come under my plaidy, and lye down beside me;
There's room in't dear lassie, believe me for twa.

Keep the Country Bonnie Lassie

This is an old reel tune which first reaches print in Bremner. A fragment of the song was collected by Herd (1776):

Keep the country, bonnie lassie,
  Keep the country, keep the country;
Keep the country, bonnie lassie;
  Lads will a' gi'e gowd for ye:
Gowd for ye, bonnie lassie,
  Gowd for ye, gowd for ye;
Keep the country, bonnie lassie;
  Lads will a' gi'e gowd for ye.

It is possible that Burns transmitted the music and verse of this title preserved in the *Museum*, as Stenhouse has said. There is, however, no trace of the tune nor the song prior to this; but this does not prove that they did not exist. Indeed it is difficult to see any justification for anyone writing the verse some seventy years after the obvious event which inspired it; although Burns did visit the Kenmure home and may have been stimulated by this.

That event was associated with the less romantic but more widespread rising for the Stewart Kings in 1715. William Gordon, Sixth Viscount Kenmure, received a commission from the Earl of Mar to raise the Jacobites in the South of Scotland in October 1715. Although the Kenmure family belonged to the North, Lochinvar to be exact, Charles I granted them a charter of land in Galloway in the south-west to which they resorted in 1629.

Setting out at the head of nearly 200 horse, Kenmure proclaimed the chevalier as James VIII in various Border towns, then marched with the rebel forces into England to become one of those who were captured, or surrendered, after the defeat at Preston.

On arrival in London, the prisoners were mounted on horseback, their arms pinioned, and led in procession with drums beating to the Tower. The mob, it is recorded, congregated to receive them with wild derision, beating warming pans and marrow-bones, etc., to swell the din. A brief trial condemned him to execution in February of the following year, to the great sorrow of his friends and those who knew him for his mild and gentle disposition and other qualities or lack of them which made him so unsuitable for military command. Indeed, tradition has it that his charger, a normally docile beast, thrice refused to let him get 'on and awa' on the fatal morn of his departure.

> O Kenmure's on and awa, Willie,
>   O Kenmure's on and awa.
> And Kenmure's lord's the bravest lord,
>   That ever Galloway saw.

Keppoch's Rant

The Keppoch Macdonalds, called the Clanranald of Lochaber, were founded in medieval times.

When Prince Charlie arrived in Moidart in 1745, Alexander Macdonald of Keppoch was probably the first to declare for him. It is worth mentioning that in the first action of the rebellion, before the standard was raised at Glenfinnan, Lochiel and Keppoch intercepted two companies of the second battalion of the Scots Royals, under the command of a Captain Scott, while on their way from Fort Augustus to reinforce Fort William. To avoid unnecessary bloodshed, Keppoch advanced alone to Scott's party, and offered them quarter, which they gratefully accepted. If Keppoch could have foreseen the cruelties to be perpetrated by that same Scott on the people of the West Highlands after Culloden where Keppoch was slain, there would have been a different tale, one thinks.

Kingussie Flower

Kingussie is a town in Inverness-shire. The dance *Kingussie Flower* was devised by David Anderson, itinerant dancing master of Dundee, in the late nineteenth century. It was one of a series of Country Dances which Anderson published and named after towns on his itinerary. Miss Milligan found the tune in a nineteenth century book, attached to a song entitled *A Bank of Flowers*.

Knit the Pocky

This is an old reel. A 'pocky' was a glove with no tops to the fingers.

Lady Baird's Reel

Lady Baird of Sauchtonhall, an estate in the environs of Edinburgh. Daniel Dow composed the tune of this name and apparently Thomas Wilson set figures to it early in the nineteenth century which provide the germ of the R.S.C.D.S. dance.

Lady Harriet Hope

The Lady Harriet Hope referred to here was probably the Lady Henrietta Johnstone, only daughter of the first Marquis of Annandale, who married the first Earl of Hopetoun in 1699. The Earl was distinguished in affairs of state, gave zealous support to the Treaty of Union, was chosen one of the sixteen Scots representative peers in the new British Parliament, and was re-elected repeatedly throughout his life. He died in 1742 in the great house — Hopetoun House, Linlithgowshire — the design of which he commissioned from Sir William Bruce, a famous architect of the time, and which was finished by Adam, an even more famous architect. This great house in the environs of Edinburgh is today open to the public and is frequently the scene of appropriate concerts and recitals. In the eighteenth century many great balls were held there by the resident family who were among the foremost patrons of music and dance in the capital.

Lady Jean Murray's Rant

It is likely that this title honours the same Lady *Jane* Murray whom we discuss under *The Countess of Crawford*. The dance is derived from the Rutherford Collection 1749-56 and the tune was published by Bremner in the 1750's. The R.S.C.D.S. has re-set the dance to Dow's *Atholl House*.

Lady Louisa Macdonald

Probably the wife of Godfrey, son of Sir Alexander Macdonald of Sleat (9th Bart. — d. 1795).

Lady Mary Menzies

The tune so named certainly existed in the 1750's but the identity of the lady honoured must remain in doubt. The family of Menzies — the 'z' indicates a liquid 'n' and hence the name should be pronounced 'Mingis' — obtained a footing in Atholl in Medieval times. The name is not Gaelic but Anglo-Norman. The seat of the family — Menzies Castle — stands in baronial dignity to the east of Loch Tay. A collection of Country Dances enjoyed by the Menzies family in the eighteenth century is preserved in the Perth library.

La Russe

This dance is a Quadrille figure and is not a Country Dance.

La Tempete

This dance was very popular in nineteenth century ballrooms everywhere and served as the finishing dance at the ball at Inverary Castle in honour of Queen Victoria in 1875. The R.S.C.D.S. version differs from others to be found in nineteenth century ballroom handbooks in minor details. In one American book I have consulted it is called *Tom-Pete*!

Laird of Dumbiedykes

The Laird of 'Damn-me-dikes', a character in Scott's novel, *The Heart of Midlothian*. He was heartless and grasping but made some concessions to remorse on his deathbed. 'Dinna let the world get a grip o' ye, Jock,' he advised his son, 'but' — he added — 'keep the gear thegither!'

Argyles bowling Green

First Couple sett, and cast off. Then sett again, and the first Man cast down and fallen 'twixt the 3d Couple; the first Woman cast up and fall in twixt the 2d Couple. Then lead three hands abreast, and then three hands up & downe & the two you had abreast. Then toes with the two you had three hands round. Then sett acrofs and turn. Then sett to your Partner, and turn. Then hands round w the 2d Couple. Then lead up and cast off.

FROM DRUMMOND CASTLE MS.

Lamb Skinnet

Lambskinit, a game of cards of German origin (c. 1687). The term comes from *Lansquenet*, a class of lance-bearing mercenary soldiers in the European campaigns of the sixteenth and seventeenth centuries.

The Lassies o' Dunse (& Laddies o' Dunse)

The Lads o' Dunse is the festive name of the citizens of the ancient town of Dunse in Berwick County, about forty miles south of Edinburgh. The Lassies o' Dunse is an obvious modification of the original term in favour of the lassies. The title of the Country Dance — *Ladies of Dunse* — may derive from a corruption of Laddies or Lassies. Whatever it may be, lads or lassies, the town boldly asserts its supremacy in its motto: *Dunse dings a'*.

Dunse early received historical notice by its being the hometown of the celebrated twelfth century scholar known on the Continent as John Duns Scotus. It is believed that the word *dunce*, applied to a dull student, arose from the sarcastic application of the old scholar's name.

The Lass o' Livingstone

This tune is described by Ramsay, who was born in 1684, as ancient. The song current in the countryside was not, in Burns' words, 'ladies' reading', although, as he also remarks, it had a great deal of poetic merit. Ramsay supplied a more genteel set of verses in 1724. The traditional verses, possibly revised by Burns, are collected in his *Merry Muses*. Here he spells Livingstone, 'Liviston', which is the common Scots pronunciation. Many poems of much greater daring are published to-day without restraint.

> The bonnie lass o' Liviston
>   Her name ye ken, her name ye ken,
> And aye the welcomer ye'll be,
>   The farther ben, the father ben.
> And she has written in her contract
>   To lie her lane, to lie her lane.

The Lea Rig

The 'lea rig' was that part of the field left in pasture. The word 'rig' comes from the old practice of dividing the land into strips varying from one-quarter to half an acre, which were shared among the tenants occupying a farm. This system went by the name of *runrig*, apparently a modification of the Gaelic *roinn-ruith* — 'division run'. (*Scottish Hist. Rev.xiii*, p. 187.).

The beautiful tune *Lea-Rig* takes its name from the song associated with it. The following fragment of the old verses has come down to us:

> I'll row thee o'er the lea-rig
>   My ain kind dearie, O!
> I'll rowe thee o'er the lea-rig,
>   My ain kind dearie, O!
> Altho' the night were ne'er sae wat,
>   And I were ne'er sae weary, O,
> I'll rowe thee o'er the lea-rig,
>   My ain kind dearie, O.

Robert Fergusson (1750-74), Burns' great forerunner and exemplar in the vernacular muse, wrote two verses and then followed Burns himself. It is a perplexing phenomenon, that tunes which Burns exalted by his lines were frequently wedded to inferior poetry in later years, and perpetuated in their new form. Doubtless this is attributable to the change in taste which increasing anglification induced. Sentimentality replaced sentiment, and genteelity robustness. And, in addition perhaps, a certain loss of ground on the part of the old language, plus loss of topicality of allusions due to change in manners and custom.

For instance, in the case of Burns' *Lea-Rig*, what was the 'ewe-bughtin' ' to a generation that had ceased to herd the sheep into pens for the night? (The 'bught' was a sheep-pen,) Or 'owsen frae the furrowed field' to a generation which had never seen oxen yoked to a plough? So it befalls that less worthy but more easily comprehensible verses have occasionally displaced Burns' in more recent song collections.

In *Lea-Rig* Burns has been somewhat uneven; his first verse is quite superb and sets a level which is hardly reached by the other two. This, doubtless, is what he felt himself, for he was not too satisfied with it.

When o'er the hill the eastern star
Tells bughtin' time is near my jo;
And owsen frae the furrowed field
　　Return sae dowf and weary, O,
Downby the burn, where scented birks
　　Wi' dew are hanging clear, my jo;
I'll meet thee on the lea-rig,
　　My ain kind dearie, O.

In mirkest glen, at midnight hour,
　　I'd rove and ne'er be eerie, O;
If thro' that glen I gaed to thee,
　　My ain kind dearie, O!
Although the night were ne'er sae wild,
　　And I were ne'er sae weary, O,
I'd meet thee on the lea-rig,
　　My ain kind dearie, O!

The hunter lo'es the morning sun,
　　To rouse the mountain deer, my jo;
At noon the fisher seeks the glen,
　　Along the burn to steer, my jo;
Gi'e me the hour o' gloamin' gray,
　　It mak's my heart sae cheerie, O,
To meet thee on the lea-rig,
　　My ain kind dearie, O.

Lennox love to Blantyre

Robert Burns had a neglected rheumatic heart condition which caught up with him in his middle thirties. Although his complaint was recognized as Rheumatic Fever, the treatment prescribed has all the appearance of being a matter of trial and mostly error. He was ultimately advised to try sea-bathing, for which purpose he moved for a time closer to the Solway Firth, not far from his home in Dumfries. This, in the circumstances, drastic treatment, was to no avail and his condition worsened. He returned home, rightly convinced that his end was near. The old fiction that he suffered from the effects of alcoholic excess took a long time to disappear. This we owe to the limited knowledge and prejudices of Dr. Currie, the early biographer of the poet.

106

To complicate matters for the poet, Mrs. Burns was expecting any day to give birth to another child. Fortunately, however, she enjoyed the voluntary assistance of Jessy Lewars, a young orphaned girl of eighteen, sister of one of Burns' colleagues on the Excise. Burns was touched by Jessy's devoted attention and no doubt was moved also by reflections on the beauty and power of young love which her diligence and presence inspired. He wrote for her the song 'Altho' thou maun never be mine' and his last great lyric:

> O, wert thou in the cauld blast,
>   On yonder lea, on yonder lea.
> My plaidie to the angry airt,
>   I'd shelter thee, I'd shelter thee.
> Or did Misfortune's bitter storms
>   Around thee blaw, around thee blaw,
> Thy bield should be my bosom
>   To share it a', to share it a'.
>
> Or were I in the wildest waste,
>   Sae black and bare, sae black and bare.
> The desert were a paradise.
>   If thou wert there, if thou wert there;
> Or were I monarch o' the globe,
>   Wi' thee to reign, wi' thee to reign;
> The brightest jewel in my crown,
>   Wad be my queen, wad be my queen.

Jessy told Dr. Chambers, the learned biographer of the poet, that Burns had called at her home one day when he was far from well, and had offered, if she would play her favourite air on the harpsichord, to write verses to it. This air was *Lennox love to Blantyre* and the verses, of course, became those quoted above.

Thomson changed the metre and printed the song to a different tune, the original tune having too great a compass for ordinary voices.

The tune, *Lennox love to Blantyre*, is possibly older than its title, which can be dated, as we shall see in 1702. It first appears in Sinkler's MS. (1710). In a characteristically Scottish way, the first theme of the tune ends in the minor and the second in the major, which gives it much flavour. It appears in print in Bremner's *Reels*, 1757, and often thereafter. The Country Dance *Lennox Love to Blantyre*, published by the R.S.C.D.S., is taken from the Holmain MS. (*c.* 1740).

'Lennox' is the name of that district which is largely embraced by the county of Dunbarton. 'Blantyre' is the name of a town in the upper valley of the Clyde. What then, it may be asked, is the meaning of 'Lennox Love to Blantyre'? For this story we must turn to the court of Charles II and the woman for whom the king almost divorced his queen, 'La Belle Stuart'. Frances Therese Stuart was the eldest daughter of Walter Stuart, third son of the First Lord Blantyre. She was a celebrated beauty whose chastity perplexed the king and those courtiers, such as the Comte de Grammont, himself of Scottish descent, who sought her favour. She was one of the three best female dancers at Court and is a familiar figure to all who have inspected a British copper coin, for she was the model for the image of Britannia. She put an end to the king's infatuation by marrying the Duke of Lennox and Richmond, although this was initially done secretly because of the Duke's estrangement from Court.

The Duke died at Elsinore in December 1672, while he was Ambassador Extraordinary to the Danish Court, and the Lennox estates and a pension were settled on the Duchess for life. By sagacious management she managed to accrue a substantial fortune which, on her death in 1702, she willed to various members of her family. The bulk of this was bestowed upon her nephew, the Fifth Lord Blantyre, with the stipulation that it be invested in a purchase of lands in the Kingdom of Scotland — 'which estate when purchased shall be called and I appoint the same to be named and called Lennoxlove', to be preserved 'in the heires male of that family soe long as the same can be done by the Lawes of that Kingdom in perpetuall remembrance of mee'.

Land was purchased, accordingly, in East Lothian, Dunbartonshire, Renfrewshire and Berwickshire. That in East Lothian was no less than Lethington, the ancient property of the Maitland family, of which William Maitland of Lethington, Secretary of State to Mary, Queen of Scots, was the most illustrious member. This estate was selected to receive the name Lennoxlove. It appears that those who were unaware of the circumstances were wont to see in this name some suggestion of favour from the Lennox family to the Blantyres and rationalized 'Lennoxlove' as an abbreviation of 'Lennox's love to Blantyre'. Hence the title of our tune and dance.

Loch Erichtside or *(Erochtside)*

Loch Ericht is a remote loch in the Perthshire highlands. The Strathspey of that name first appears in McGlashan's *Reels* (1786) as *Loch Eireachd Side*. It is a set of the tune associated with the song 'I'm o'er young to marry yet'. The Country Dance was collected in the Borders by Jamieson, but whether it was the dance of the same name which Burns performed with a jovial party on Loch Lomondside during his return from his tour of the Highlands in 1786, we have no way of knowing.

There are several lyrics set to this tune: Burns' 'Young Peggy blooms' and 'O stay, sweet warbling woodlark', and Lady Nairn's better-known 'The Lass of Gowrie'.

'Twas on a simmer's afternoon,
A wee before the sun gaed down,
My lassie, wi' a braw new gown,
   Cam' o'er the hills to Gowrie.
The rosebud tinged wi' morning show'r,
Blooms fresh within the sunny bow'r,
But Katie was the fairest flow'r
   That ever bloomed in Gowrie.

Lochiel (Lochiel's awa tae France) (Lochiel's Rant)

The Camerons, originally a clan in Lochaber, in the Central Highlands, obtained a charter of the barony of Lochiel 'de Knoydart' in the thirteenth century. This territory and the lands of Glenloy and Locharkaig, purchased by Sir Ewen Cameron in the reign of Charles II, are still in the possession of the family. Cameron of Lochiel is the chief of Clan Cameron and in virtue of several distinguished predecessors, notably Sir Ewen mentioned above and Sir Ewen's grandson, carries a name distinguished in the romance of Scotland.

Sir Ewen (1629 - 1719), familiarly known in Gaelic as Mac-'onnuill Dhu — the 'son of Black Donald', was brought up at Inveraray by his kinsman, the Marquis of Argyll, but lived to support resistance to Cromwell's occupation and support the cause of the exiled Stewarts, beginning with Charles II, which inevitably placed him on sides contrary to those of his former guardian. Such was the fierceness and persistence of the Camerons of Lochiel, that Cromwell came to terms with them rather than face continued strife.

109

It is no surprise to find Sir Ewen in 1689 disdaining the offer of a title from King William of Orange and of bribes to gain his neutrality when Viscount Dundee — 'Bonnie Dundee' — raised the standard of the deposed King James. Nor that he and his men were first in the fray at the Battle of Killiecrankie in which Dundee's army routed that of the Government. He was an old man of eighty-six, however, when the Earl of Mar raised the standard for the 'King ower the water' in 1715, and had to leave that adventure to the attention of his son John.

His grandson, Donald, was to play a role in the later rebellion (1745) and in the history of his people, that makes a rival claim on our remembrance. He exerted himself to improve the living habits and condition of his clan and was much respected on this account and for his genial disposition. The 'Gentle Lochiel' he was called.

Since Donald's father was still alive, he was known as 'young' Lochiel. He was involved in the deliberations in the 1740's to restore the Stewarts to the throne, but was against any attempt being made without foreign assistance. Young Lochiel's influence with the clans was recognized by the Pretender, who invested him with power to negotiate on his behalf with his supporters in Scotland, and when Prince Charlie landed at Borodale, in Moidart, it was primarily to make contact with Lochiel.

Lochiel proceeded to the rendezvous determined to dissuade the Prince from his intention in the absence of troops and arms. On his way he called on his brother, John Cameron of Fassifern, who advised him not to go in person, but to send a letter. 'Brother,' he said, 'I know you better than you know yourself. If this prince once set eyes upon you he will make you do whatever he pleases.' But Lochiel could not think of this; he must, he thought, wait upon his Prince and give his reasons for not joining him face to face. This he did, and was resolute in his stand until the Prince challenged his high sense of chivalry by declaring that he would take the field regardless of the strength of his adherents — 'Lochiel, who, my father has often told me, was our firmest friend, may stay at home, and from the newspapers learn of the fate of his prince!'

This was too much for Lochiel; his own sentiments and the whole weight of the heroic tradition of his family were thrown against his better judgement, and he relented. By supporting the Prince, he drew others to the standard and made possible the rebellion and all its consequences, good and bad. There were noble qualities in Lochiel that even his foes had to respect, epitomizing in his person the humanity and restraint that characterized the

110

conduct of the victorious Highland 'rabble'. Their distinguished place in the romantic annals of their people is in some measure due to this. At least they left no blemish. What a contrast to the brutality of their adversaries when the tide of battle ultimately turned against them at Culloden. No quarter in pursuit, families and friends exposed, defenceless, to the avenging dragoons. The wounded denied succour where they lay on the battlefield; not even water could be carried to them by those moved to compassion by the piteous entreaties. Then, on the third day, all who remained alive were shot where they lay. For this, the Duke of Cumberland, brother of George III, was responsible, and for this and other brutalities, his name deservedly lives in infamy.

Lochiel represents something else, and Scotland can be proud of him. He survived Culloden, although severely wounded in both ankles, being carried from the field by his people. About two months later, at a rendezvous in Rannoch, he was attended by Sir Stewart Thriepland, an Edinburgh physician, after which he joined Cluny MacPherson and some other distinguished fugitives in the Badenoch country. After about five months, they were joined by the Prince who owed much to people like Kingsburgh in Skye who did not go out with him but who risked their all to aid his escape. In September 1746, the Prince, Lochiel and nearly a hundred survivors of his party were taken up by two French frigates and conducted safely to France.

One can imagine the word at last passing from glen to glen and at length to the Jacobite circles in the capital — 'Lochiel's awa tae France'. There would be much rejoicing one imagines.

The 'Gentle Lochiel' was given the command of a regiment of his expatriated countrymen but survived only a further two years, dying in 1748.

The Strathspey *Lochiel's Rant* was published by Bremner.

111

Loch Leven Castle

Loch Leven Castle is situated on an island in Loch Leven in Kinross. There is another Loch Leven in the West Highlands and the original name of Loch Lomond was Loch Leven. The word 'leven' appears to be from Gaelic roots meaning elmwood. 'Lomond' is a hill name, possibly a compound of *leamh*, elmwood, and *monadh*, mountain. Thus we have Lomond, the 'elmwood mountain'.

It is striking that in the East, the hills overlooking Loch Leven are called the 'Lomonds', and in the West, the mountain dominating another Loch Leven is called Ben Lomond. Both presumably regions of elmwood forest centuries ago.

The latter Loch Leven became known as Loch Lomond around the fourteenth century, forsaking its old name and taking the name of the mountain for some reason. In both East and West, a river Leven drains the loch, and indeed, Loch Lomond is in the region of Lennox — from Levanaux, 'elm field' — roughly the modern Dunbartonshire.

However, Loch Leven Castle, long a ruin, once belonged to the Douglas family and gains its distinction from having confined within its walls the twenty-four-year-old Mary, Queen of Scots, in 1568. Mary, having married Bothwell, her bold abductor, faced opposition from the Protestant party and from the enemies of Bothwell. To make a fascinating and turbulent story short, the opposition succeeded in capturing her and imprisoning her in Loch Leven Castle. Bothwell escaped to Scandinavia.

During her period in the castle, she was obliged to sign an instrument of abdication, the Earl of Moray, her half-brother, becoming regent.

After eleven months, she escaped with the help of a youth of the Douglas family, who obtained the keys of the castle. The tale forms an exciting part of Sir Walter Scott's novel *The Abbot*. Nothing concerning Mary, Queen of Scots, is without the greatest interest. She was a most exceptional person, a young woman of true greatness, an ornament to her time and to Scotland's harshness. How much the richer Scotland is for having belonged to her.

Lucy Campbell

A tune entitled *Acharnac's Reel* in Cumming the Strathspey fiddler's *Collection* (1780), appears as *Louisa Campbell's Delight* in McGlashan's *Strathspeys* and in the Gow Collection as *Lucy Campbell*. The identity of Lucy or Louisa cannot easily be ascertained. It may only be a coincidence that a Country Dance bearing the same name as the tune in Gow was found contained in the old book of Scottish-Irish dances from which the R.S.C.D.S. has restored the dance.

In any case, the Society has set the dance to a reel composed by the great Robert Mackintosh – the *Hon. Mrs. Campbell (of Lochnell)* rather than to the Strathspey named *Lucy Campbell*.

Lord Rosslyn's Fancy

This dance and tune are named after the first Lord Rosslyn created in 1801. He was Alexander Wedderburn (1733-1805), who after being admitted advocate in Scotland at the early age of nineteen moved to England where he was called to the bar in 1757. He became attorney-general and in 1773 united with Lord North in forming a celebrated coalition ministry. On its dissolution he joined the opposition. As one obituarist remarked, 'He could argue with great ingenuity on either side, so that it was difficult to anticipate his future by his past opinions' — his 'fancy' indeed.

The Machine Without Horses

In solving the riddle of this title we must take note of two facts. One, that the dance and the tune are taken from a publication of the year 1772 — long before the advent of the steam carriage or steam locomotive, and two, that the word 'machine' was often used of a horse-drawn carriage in Scotland. The 'Machine without horses', then, could well be the carriage without the horses, and it has been suggested that the figures of the dance are intended to represent the parts of the carriage — the wheels, the shafts and the passenger compartment. This is very plausible and very likely, but I, personally, have been very hesitant about drawing such conclusions since an experience I had not long ago with a dance devised by my friend Bob Campbell of Ontario, entitled *Over the Sea to the West*.

"In the Old Assembly Close"
Drawn by W.B. Hole, ARSA.

This dance was inspired by the theme of emigration, and one evening I commended Bob on his success with it and on his ingenious combination of motifs. I was not a little surprised when he appeared puzzled and said, 'What motifs?'

114

'Well,' said I, 'there are the waves, the shape of the ship, the wheels symbolizing the engines or paddles, the disembarkation of the passengers — it is all there.'

Bob was intrigued by this, as, he alleged, such ideas had never entered his head! The reader can judge whether some psychic influence was not at work in this instance. But if it means that we must be sceptical about the interpretation of *Machine without Horses*, we are left to accept that the term simply alludes to the carriage without the horses or, and this is an interesting idea, that it refers to the sedan chair!

The sedan chair comprised a closed cabin supported on trams or poles fore and aft, held by two liveried porters or 'chairmen'. In Glasgow and Edinburgh, these chairmen were usually Highlanders. They were the same people who performed the official function of running errands, delivering messages or parcels and the like, the famous 'caddies'. There were stands of sedan chairs just as there are taxi-stands to-day, and likewise there were private sedan chairs just as there are chauffeur-driven cars to-day. The last private sedan chair in Edinburgh, it is said, was owned by Lady Don, one of the Buccleuch Place Dance Assembly directresses of whom Cockburn writes in his *Memorials*.

The sedan, then, was exactly analogous to the modern taxi-cab in the principal burghs of eighteenth century Scotland. It had first appeared in London early in the previous century, and we can assume that it was some years later in making its debut in Edinburgh. We do know, however, that there were only a few hackney coaches in Edinburgh in 1689 and this situation changed little until about one hundred years later.

Throughout most of the eighteenth century, then, the sedan chair reigned supreme but was fast disappearing by the turn of the nineteenth century. In 1800, there were no more than two dozen in Glasgow. Their great merit was their indifference to the hazardous surfaces of the streets and their convenience for negotiating narrow lanes and closes. In the dark they were often preceded by a servant carrying a flambeau or oil flare, and often, if the freight were a lady returning from an evening ball or assembly, or concert, she would be accompanied by her escort who walked alongside.

In Glasgow, around the end of the eighteenth century, the sedan chairs were extensively kept by one William Moses who was accustomed to join his servants in being the bearer of a lady in one of his sedans to an assembly, dressing himself in the first style of fashion. If the lady had no partner, Strang tells us, he introduced her to one, or danced with her himself. He became very rich and purchased property near the village — as it was then — of Springburn, naming it 'Mosesfield'. So he became, as he styled himself, William Moses of Mosesfield!

There was very inadequate street lighting by the year 1800. Here and there, perhaps, the feeble flickering of a few oil lamps on elevated wooden pedestals which were ignited by the town lamplighters, frequently followed by a group of skipping chanting children as they were a century later:

> Leerie, leerie, licht the lamps
>   Lang legs and crookit shanks;
> Kill a louse — catch a flea;
>   Hing leerie ower the brae!

Ten was a late hour in these days and dinner parties were held at four. The sedan chair comporting its single fare may pass the occasional matrons and ladies returning from tea, picking their way in high-heeled pattens along the streets, preceded by their chambermaids carrying the three-cornered oil lantern called a 'Bouet' and curtseying at each puddle or 'dub' to be avoided in their path. The sedan removed such concerns, provided safety and shelter and stalwart company. The 'machine without horses' indeed, to the men from the glens and the isles. How else would they describe it?

Madge Wildfire

The name Madge Wildfire comes from a character — or the disguise of a character — in the novel, *The Heart of Midlothian*. George Staunton, alias George Robertson, 'Gentleman Geordie', was the accomplice of Wilson the smuggler. Scott has him take the disguise of a woman and call himself Madge Wildfire, to lead the rioters who took revenge on Captain Porteous, of the Edinburgh town guard, for the irresponsible killing of several of the bystanders at Wilson's hanging. Sharpe, the antiquarian, recorded that 'People of high rank were concerned in the affair. My great-grandfather, Lord Alva, told my grandfather that many of the mob were persons of rank — some of them disguised as women. Lord Haddington, for one, in his cook-maid's dress.' (Wilson: *Reminiscences of Old Edinburgh*.)

This famous incident of the people taking the law into their

116

own hands occurred in 1736 and is known to historians as the 'Porteous Riots' or 'Porteous Mob'. Perhaps some description of the incident would be welcome. It is certainly exciting to read the words of an eye-witness of some of the incidents, especially when the witness was none other than a great dancer and reminiscer, Alexander ('Jupiter') Carlyle, in his *Autobiography*:

> I was witness to a very extraordinary scene that happened in the month of February or March 1736, which was the escape of Robertson, a condemned criminal, from the Tolbooth Church in Edinburgh. In those days it was usual to bring the criminals who were condemned to death into that church, to attend public worship every Sunday after their condemnation, when the clergyman made some part of his discourse and prayers to suit their situation; which, among other circumstances of solemnity which then attended the state of condemned criminals, had no small effect on the public mind. Robertson and Wilson were smugglers, and had been condemned for robbing a custom-house where some of their goods had been deposited; a crime which at that time did not seem, in the opinion of the common people, to deserve so severe a punishment. I was carried by an acquaintance to Church to see the prisoners on the Sunday before the day of execution. We went early into the church on purpose to see them come in, and were seated in a pew before the gallery in front of the pulpit. Soon after we went into the church by the door from the Parliament Close, the criminals were brought in by the door next the Tolbooth, and placed in a long pew, not far from the pulpit. Four soldiers came in with them, and placed Robertson at the head of the pew, and Wilson below him, two of themselves sitting below Wilson, and two in a pew behind him.
>
> The bells were ringing and the doors were open, while the people were coming into the church. Robertson watched his opportunity, and suddenly springing up, got over the pew into the passage that led in to the door in the Parliament Close, and no person offering to lay hands on him, made his escape in a moment — so much the more easily, perhaps, as everybody's attention, was drawn to Wilson, who was a stronger man, and who, attempting to follow Robertson, was seized by the soldiers and struggled so long with them that the two who at last followed Robertson were too late. It was reported that he had maintained that he might let his companion have time. That might be his second thought, but his first was certainly to escape himself, for I saw him set his foot on the seat to leap over, when the soldiers pulled him back. Wilson was immediately carried out to the Tolbooth, and Robertson, getting uninterrupted through the Parliament Square, down the back stairs, into the Cowgate, was heard no more till he arrived in Holland. This was an interesting scene, and by filling the public mind with compassion for the unhappy person who did not escape, and who was the better charac-

The Porteous Riots

ter of the two, had probably some influence in producing what followed: for when the sentence against Wilson came to be executed a few weeks thereafter, a very strong opinion prevailed that there was a plot to force the Town Guard, whose duty it is to attend executions under the order of a civil magistrate.

There was a Captain Porteous, who by his good behaviour in the army had obtained a subaltern's commission, and had afterwards, when on half-pay, been preferred to the command of the City Guard. This man, by his skill in manly exercises, particularly the golf, and by his gentlemanly behaviour, was admitted into the company of his superiors, which elated his mind, and added insolence to his native roughness, so that he was much hated and feared by the mob of Edinburgh. When the day of execution came, the rumour of a deforcement at the gallows prevailed strongly; and the Provost and Magistrates (not in their own minds very strong) thought it a good measure to apply for three or four companies of a marching regiment that lay in the Canongate, to be drawn up in the Lawnmarket, a street leading from the Tolbooth to the Grassmarket, the place of execution, in order to overawe the mob by their being at hand. Porteous, who, it is said, had his natural courage increased to rage by any suspicion that he and his Guard could not execute the law, and being heated likewise with wine — for he had dined, as the custom then was, between one and two — became perfectly furious when he passed by the three companies drawn up in the street as he marched along with his prisoner.

Mr. Baille had taken windows in a house on the north side of the Grassmarket, for his pupils and me, in the second floor, about seventy or eighty yards westward of the place of execution, where we went in due time to see the show; to which I had no small aversion, having seen one at Dumfries, the execution of Jock Johnstone, which shocked me very much.

When we arrived at the house, some people who were looking from the windows were displaced, and went to a window in the common stair, about two feet below the level of ours. The street is long and wide, and there was a very great crowd assembled. The execution went on with the usual forms, and Wilson behaved in a manner very becoming his situation. There was not the least appearance of an attempt to rescue; but soon after the executioner had done his duty, there was an attack made upon him, as usual on such occasions, by the boys and blackguards throwing stones and dirt in testimony of their abhorrence of the hangman. But there was no attempt to break through the guard and cut down the prisoner. It was generally said that there was very little, if any, more violence than had usually happened on such occasions. Porteous, however, inflamed with wine and jealousy, thought proper to order his Guard to fire, their muskets being loaded with slugs; and when the soldiers showed reluctance, I saw him turn to them with threatening gesture and an inflamed countenance. They obeyed, and fired; but wishing to do as little harm as possible, many of them elevated their pieces, the effect of which was that some people were wounded in the windows; and one unfortunate lad, whom we had displaced, was killed in the stair window by a slug entering his head. His name was Henry Black, a journeyman tailor, whose bride was the daughter of the house we were in. She fainted away when he was brought into the house speechless, where he only lived till nine or ten o'clock. We had seen many people, women and men, fall on the street, and at first thought it was only through fear, and by their crowding on one another to escape. But when the crowd dispersed, we saw them lying dead or wounded, and had no longer any doubt of what had happened. The numbers were said to be eight or nine killed, and double the number wounded; but this was never exactly known.

This unprovoked slaughter irritated the common people to the last; and the state of grief and rage into which their minds were thrown, was visible in the high commotion that appeared in the multitude. Our tutor was very anxious to have us all safe in our lodgings, but durst not venture out to see if it was practicable to go home. I offered to go; went, and soon returned, offering to conduct them safe to our lodgings, which were only half-way down the Lawnmarket, by what was called the Castle Wynd, which was just at hand, to the westward. There we remained safely, and were not allowed to stir out any more that night till about nine o'clock, when, the streets having long been quiet, we all grew anxious to learn the fate of Henry Black, and I was allowed to go back to the house. I took the younger Maxwell with me, and found that he had expired an hour before we arrived. A single slug had penetrated the side of his head an inch above the ear. The sequel of this affair was, that Porteous was tried and condemned to be hanged; but by the intercession of some of the Judges themselves, who thought his case hard, he was reprieved by the Queen-Regent. The Magistrates, who on this occasion, as on the former, acted weakly, designed to have removed him to the Castle for greater security. But a plot was laid and conducted by some persons unknown with the greatest secrecy, policy, and vigour, to prevent that design, by forcing the prison the night before, and executing the sentence upon him themselves, which to effectuate cost them from from eight at night till two in the morning; they met with no interruption, though there were five companies of a marching regiment lying in the Canongate.

This happened on the 7th of September 1736; and so prepossessed were the minds of every person that something extraordinary would take place that day, that I at Prestonpans, nine miles from Edinburgh, dreamt that I saw Captain Porteous hanged in the Grassmarket. I got up betwixt six and seven, and went to my father's servant, who was thrashing in the barn which lay on the roadside leading to Aberlady and North Berwick, who said that several men on horseback had passed about five in the morning, whom having asked for news, they replied there was none, but that

120

Captain Porteous had been dragged out of prison, and hanged on a dyer's tree at two o'clock that morning.

This bold and lawless deed not only provoked the Queen, who was Regent at the time, but gave some uneasiness to Government. It was represented as a dangerous plot, and was ignorantly connected with a great meeting of zealous Covenanters, of whom many still remained in Galloway and the west, which had been held in summer, in Pentland Hills, to renew the Covenant. But this was a mistake; for the murder of Porteous had been planned and executed by a few of the relations or friends of those whom he had slain; who, being of a rank superior to mere mob, had carried on their design with so much secrecy, ability, and steadiness as made it be ascribed to a still higher order, who were political enemies to Government. This idea provoked Lord Isla, (Archibald, brother of John, Fourth Duke of Argyle, who succeeded to the Dukedom in 1743), who then managed the affairs of Scotland under Sir Robert Walpole, to carry through an Act of Parliament in next session for the discovery of the murderers of Captain Porteous, to be published by reading it for twelve months, every Sunday forenoon, in all the churches in Scotland, immediately after divine service, or rather in the middle of it for the minister was ordained to read it between the lecture and the sermon, two discourses usually given at that time. This clause, it was said, was intended to purge the Church of fanatics, for as it was believed that most clergymen of that description would not read the Act, they would become liable to the penalty, which was deposition. By good-luck for the clergy, there was another party distinction among them (besides that occasioned by their ecclesiastical differences), viz. that of Argathelian and Squadrone, of which political divisions there were some both of the high-flying and moderate clergy. Some very sensible men of the latter class having discovered the design of the Act, either by information or sagacity, convened meetings of clergy at Edinburgh, and formed resolutions, and carried on correspondence through the Church to persaude as many as possible to disobey the Act, that the great number of offenders might secure the safety of the whole. This was actually the case, for as one-half of the clergy, at least, disobeyed in one shape or other, the idea of inflicting the penalty was dropped altogether. In the meantime, the distress and perplexity which this Act occasioned in many families of the clergy, was of itself a cruel punishment for a crime in which they had no hand. The anxious days and sleepless nights which it occasioned to such ministers as had families, and at the same time scruples about the lawfulness of reading the Act, were such as no one could imagine who had not witnessed the scene.

The part my grandfather took was manly and decided; for, not thinking the reading of the Act unlawful, he pointedly obeyed. My father was very scrupulous, being influenced by Mr. Erskine of Grange, and other enemies of Sir Robert Walpole. On the other hand, the good sense of his wife, and the consideration of eight or nine children whom he then had, and who were in danger of being turned out on the world, pulled him very hard on the side of obedience. A letter from my grandfather at last settled his mind, and he read the Act.

What seemed extraordinary, after all the anxiety of Government, and the violent means they took to make a discovery, not one of these murderers was ever found. Twenty years afterwards, two or three persons returned from different parts of the world, who were supposed to be of the number; but, so far as I heard, they never disclosed themselves.

The Maid of the Mill

The *Maid of the Mill* was the name of a play, based upon Richardson's popular novel *Pamela*, by Isaac Bickerstaff (1735 - 1812), and first produced in London in 1765. It was styled a 'Comic Opera', but the lyrics are widely spaced in the action. Doubtless the joyful jig bearing the name of the play was a favourite air utilized in it. I have discovered the tune in a MS. dated 1740 in which it is entitled *Welsh Fusiliers*.

Maggie Lauder

The seventeenth century poem *Maggie Lauder* was written by Frances Semple of Beltrees, Renfrewshire, whose father, Robert, and grandfather James, were poets in a similar vein. All used the Scots vernacular rather than the English literary language in their most characteristic works, and drew their inspiration from rural characters and situations. Grandfather James (1565-1626) was the son of John Semphill 'the dancer' of the Court of Mary, Queen of Scots, and one of her 'Maries' — Mary Livingston, 'the lusty' (fair). The appellations are John Knox's.

James shared part of his education with King James VI under the celebrated historian and Latin poet, George Buchanan, and later acted as that King's amanuensis and served as Ambassador to the English Court (1599) and France, before the union of the Kingdoms. His principal contribution to Scottish poetry is *The Packman's Paternoster*, later supplemented by his son Robert, whose most influential poem was the elegy of Habbie Simpson, *The Piper of Kilbarchan*. 'Influential' because its metre became a favourite of both Fergusson and Burns, and seems peculiarly suitable for the rhythms of teutonic Scots speech.

To Frances (*c.* 1616-82) have been ascribed the authorship of these rollicking works — *She rose and let me in*, *Hallow Fair*, *The Blythsome Bridal* and *The Banishment of Poverty*, as well as *Maggie Lauder*.

Francis Semple is our earliest authority for the persons of Maggie Lauder and 'Rob the Ranter'. It is possible that he drew upon some fragment of song or metrical tale current in the countryside, as so many later Scottish poets have done, but there is no trace of it. The 'Anster Fair' mentioned in the poem was a notable fair held in eastern Anstruther, on the Fife coast, on the first Tuesdays after April 11, July 5 and November 12.

A more recent poem (early nineteenth century) written by William Tennant, may be known to the reader, in which Maggie Lauder is made contemporaneous with James V (early sixteenth century), but this is no more than the poet's conjecture.

The air, along with many other Scottish airs, made its way to London in the early eighteenth century, and was used, according to Stenhouse, in *The Quaker's Opera*, performed at Lee and Harper's booth in Bartholomew Fair, 1728, and in Gay's *Achilles*, 1733. The same authority also tells us that the air had previously been used for a song called 'Sally's New Answer, set to the tune of Mogey Lauther', a parody on Crey's 'Sally in our Alley'.

Francis Semple's verses are subjoined:

Wha wadna be in love
  Wi' bonnie Maggie Lauder?
A piper met her gaun tae Fife,
  And spier'd what was't they ca'd her:
Richt scornfully she answered him,
  Begone, ye hallanshaker!
Jog on your gate, you bladderskate!
  My name is Maggie Lauder.

Maggie! quoth he; now by my bags,
  I'm fidgin fain to see thee!
Sit down by me, my bonnie bird,
  In troth I winna steer thee;
For I'm a piper to my trade,
  My name is Rab the Ranter:
The lasses loup as they were daft,
  When I blaw up my chanter.

Piper, quo Meg, hae ye your bags,
  An' is your drone in order?
If ye be Rab, I've heard o' you;
  Live you upon the Border?
The lasses a', baith far and near,
  Have heard o' Rab the Ranter,
I'll shake my fuit wi' right gude will,
  Gif ye'll blaw up your chanter.

Then to his bags he flew wi' speed;
  About the drone he twisted:
Meg up and wallop'd ower the green;
  For brawly could she frisk it!
Weel done! quo he. Play up! quo she,
  Weel bobbed! quo Rab the Ranter;
It's worth my while to play, indeed,
  When I hae sic a dancer!

Weel hae ye play'd your part! quo Meg;
  Your cheeks are like the crimson!
There's nane in Scotland plays sae weel,
  Sin' we lost Habbie Simpson
I've lived in Fife, baith maid and wife,
  This ten years and a quarter;
Gin ye should come to Anster Fair,
  Spier ye for Maggie Lauder.

The Marchioness of Blandford's Reel

The Country Dance of this name is taken from Campbell's *Collection*, 1794. If the title is a guide, it is English, as there is no Scottish tune of that name. With that we could dismiss it here were it not for the fact that the R.S.C.D.S. has attached the *Countess of Loudon's Reel* to the dance. The importance of this to us is that the Countess of Loudon referred to here would undoubtedly be that Countess who carried the title in her own right after the death of her husband, the Fifth Earl, in the 1780's. In which case, we are dealing with none other than Flora MacLeod of Raasay of whom Boswell wrote so glowingly in his *Tour of the Hebrides*, and to whom we refer under *Mrs. MacLeod of Raasay*. The worthy subject of a Scottish dance indeed! What a pity the R.S.C.D.S. does not hold to the original system of naming the dance after the tune in this case. There is no Scottish sentiment attached to the Marchioness of Blandford that I know of.

I regret that I have not been able to determine who composed the jig called the *Countess of Loudon's Reel*. However, it is an odd commentary on life that the daughter of a man who had given succour to Prince Charlie should marry the son of a man who led an army against him.

The Marquis of Blandford is the title taken by the oldest son of the Duke of Marlborough.

Marquis of Huntly's Highlanders

The Earldom of Huntly was conferred in 1449 on the oldest son of Alexander de Seton, descendant of a sister of Robert de Bruce, and his wife, Elizabeth de Gordon. The Norman antecedents are indicated by the names. The Sixth Earl was created a Marquis in 1599 at a time when he was in high favour at Court where he and the King, according to Calderwood (*History vi*, p.100) 'passed over the time with drinking and waughting'. The attachment of the First Marquis to the Church of Rome involved him and his family in a great deal of trouble in a century of trouble — the seventeenth.

The territory of this family — Strathspey, Strathbogie, Aboyne, Strathaven, Glenlivet, Badenoch, and environs, crowded with association with Scottish dance and dance music, and comprising that region commonly known as the North-East, was studded with their fortified residences, and dominated by their policies. This strength came into conflict with King and Presbytery at various times in the course of history, and there were notable holders of the title and many less notable. Too many, with their ramifications, to be considered here.

Huntly, then, was a power to be reckoned with; 'Cock o' the North' as he was called, overshadowing his near neighbours, the Earls of Moray, Errol and Angus, and to be equated with the Earl of Argyll and the Duke of Hamilton in the South.

The family survived the usual vicissitudes of our historic noble families. The gallant Second Marquis languished in prison for two years, when infirm and aged, only to be executed in 1649, with but a short time left his natural life, for supporting King Charles I. Here was malice, one thinks. He contributed to his own fate as well as the King's by allowing resentment at a former injury and jealousy of Montrose to impede his effective support of his cause.

However, the Restoration came and the second of his surviving sons was created Earl of Aboyne (1660) and George, Fourth Marquis, was created the First Duke of Gordon in 1684, after which the title 'Marquis of Huntly' was borne by the eldest son of the Duke of Gordon. When this dukedom became extinct in 1836, the titles of Marquis of Huntly, etc., reverted to the Earl of Aboyne.

Although, as would be expected of a family which so long adhered to the Catholic and Royalist causes, the Gordons were on the Pretender's side in 1715, the Second Duke's wife raised her children as Protestants after the Duke's death in 1728. Of these children, only the third son, Lewis, declared for the Prince in 1745 and was consequently an exile until his death in France in 1754. He was the subject of the song *O send Lewie Gordon hame* by Dr. Alexander Geddes (1737-1802), who officiated as a priest in different parts of the North of Scotland.

125

O send Lewie Gordon hame,
And the lad I daurna name;
Though his back be at the wa',
Here's to him that's far awa' !
　Ochon, my Highlandman!
　O my bonny Highlandman !
　Weel would I my true love ken,
　Amang ten thousand Highlandmen.

O! to see his tartan trews,
Bonnet blue, and laigh-heel'd shoes,
Philabeg aboon his knee!
That's the lad that I'll gang wi'.
　Ochon, my Highlandman ! etc.

The 'lad I daurna name', of course, is Prince Charlie. The tune of this song was *Tarry Woo*.

The eldest son of the Fourth Earl of Aboyne, Lord Strathaven (b. 1761), as he was called, had a vigorous military career. In 1783 he visited France, and became a popular figure at the Court of Louis XVI in virtue of his gaiety of personality and skill in dancing! He was the original 'gay Gordon', and he it was who fell heir to the patrinomy of the Gordons and the Marquisate of Huntly.

The Fourth Duke of Gordon is of special interest to us, apart from his raising important regiments including the Gordon Highlanders, as the composer of verses to the tune *Cauld Kail*, and as the employer of the most distinguished of Scotland's composers of Strathspeys — William Marshall, whose *Marquis of Huntly's Farewell*, *Miss Admiral Gordon* and *Rothiemurchus Rant*, are immortal in the annals of Scottish dance music. But this is not all; his choice of the brilliant Jane Maxwell for wife ensured his place at the centre of fashionable life and wherever fiddlesticks were 'rositted' for the dance assembly, be it London, Edinburgh, Aberdeen or Inverness, or the cottage at Kinrara (see *Duchess of Gordon*).

The Marquis of Huntly's Highland Fling was a tune composed by George Jenkins who died in 1806, and a solo dance of that name was known in the early nineteenth century, of which a record was left in the Hill MS.

126

The Menzies' Rant

The Gaelic name of this is *Ruidhle daoine na Marachan — Reel of the Menzies Men*, a Highland Reel tune. It is called *The Menzies' Rant* in the Menzies MS. (1749) from which the R.S.-C.D.S. has reconstituted the dance.

The word 'Menzies' is pronounced 'ming-is', the 'z' serving to indicate a liquid consonant preceding it. The same occurs in 'Dalzell' — 'Dayell' or D'el, and 'Mackenzie' — 'Macinyie', etc.

Merrily Danced the Quaker's Wife

In a letter to Thomson, June 30th, 1793, Burns writes:

> You know Fraser, the Hautboy player in Edinburgh? — He is here, instructing a band of Music for a Fencible Corps quartered in this country. — Among many of his airs that pleases me, there is one, well known as a Reel by the name of, 'The Quaker's Wife'; and which I remember a grand Aunt of mine used to sing, by the name of 'Liggeram cosh, my bonnie wee lass'. — Mr. Fraser plays it slow, and with an expression that quite charms me — I got such an enthusiast in it, that I made a Song for it, which I here subjoin; and inclose Fraser's set of the tune — '.

In another letter to Thomson, October 29, 1793, he writes:

> I am pleased that you are reconciled to the air of the Quaker's wife; though by the by, an old Highland gentleman and a deep Antiquarian, tells me that it is a Gaelic air, and known by the name of 'Leiger m' choss'.'

Burns confirms his previous comment that it bears that name in the West country, corrupted to Liggeram Coss. The surviving fragment is:

> Leiger m' choss, my bonnie wee lass,
> Leiger m' choss, my Dearie;
> A' the lee-lang winter night,
> Leiger m' choss, my Dearie.

The tune is in Bremner as *Merrily danced the Quaker*, and Burns supplied more than one set of words. The set he himself admired was the one he refers to in his first letter above, 'Blythe hae I been on yon hill'.

Blythe hae I been on yon hill
  As the lambs before me,
Careless ilka thought, and free
  As the breeze flew o'er me;
Now nae langer sport and play,
  Mirth or sang can please me;
Lesley is sae fair and coy,
  Care and anguish seize me.

Heavy, heavy is the task,
  Hopeless love declaring;
Trembling, I dow nocht but glow'r,
  Sighing, dumb despairing!
If she winna ease the thraws
  In my bosom swelling,
Underneath the grass-green sod
  Soon maun be my dwelling.

The Quaker's Wife is a jig and was known as a solo dance or 'twasome' in the late eighteenth century. The Country Dance is another of those which survived to be collected in the Borders.

Although the Quakers as a sect began in England, there was a considerable group of them in the North-East of Scotland by the late seventeenth century. Nicol writes in his diary — 'Great numbers of that damnable sect of the Quakers, who, being deluded by Satan, drew away mony to their profession, both men and women.' Another contemporary writes — 'They, in a furious way, cry down both ministry and magistry. Some of them seem actually possessed by a devel; their fury, their irrational passions, and convulsions are so great.' (*Baillie's Letters*, *iii*, p.323, quoted R. Chambers *Dom. Annals* vii.)

In the year 1656 it was noted that quaker doctrines were spreading and their propounders more confident. We read of Walter Scott of Raeburn, being converted to Quakerism in 1666 and being jailed in the Tolbooth of Edinburgh for this defection. His well-meaning relations were concerned that he was exposed there to others 'hardened in his pernicious opinions'. But, more important, they petitioned to have his children placed in the care of his brother, Scott of Harden, to 'be educated in the true religion'. Raeburn was moved to the Tolbooth at Jedburgh nearer his home 'where his friends and others may have occasion to convert him'. He was released four years later, restricted to his own lands and forbidden contact with any other Quaker.

His children were now at school in Glasgow, but the younger son, Walter, lived instead to become a Jacobite! This boy was great-grandfather of the great Sir Walter who alludes to this story through the medium of Jedediah Cleishbotham in the Introduction to the *Heart of Midlothian*. Perhaps, too, this was in his mind when he introduces a group of Quakers to 'Red-gauntlet' and has the fiddler, Wandering Willie, play *Merrily Danced the Quaker's Wife* in allusion to circumstances of the story.

In 1683 we find the Bishop of Aberdeen complaining of the 'insolency' of the Quakers in his diocese, erecting meeting houses, and providing schools and even burial grounds for their use. (*Privy Council Records*, quoted R. Chambers *op. cit.* vii, p. 447.)

It is difficult now to conceive the superstitious horror with which Quakers were regarded by orthodox Presbyterians in these days. Of course the same persecution led to the sailing of the *May flower* from England with all its historic consequences earlier in the century. It is certainly a peculiar conflict in which the Kirk resents the presumption of an independent sect to preach the same prognostications of doom to the sinful. Of course, it was the old story of Joan of Arc over again: like Joan, the Quaker preachers claimed direction from God. Peden the 'prophet' recognized a competitor and claimed to see a raven sit successively on the heads of a number of the sect on one occasion as they spoke in his presence. Here was confirmation of the Devil's work (Walker's *Life of Peden*).

The enlightenment of the eighteenth century is well marked by the notice in the *Edinburgh Courier* in February 18, 1725: 'We hear that a Quaker woman is encouraged by our magistrates, in her proposal of setting up a woolen manufactory in this city, and obliging herself to employ all the strolling beggars in work, and to give them food and raiment'. And in September 1729: 'The Quakers are building a place of worship in Peebles' Wynd. Though it be roofed, there is yet no window in it; but some merrily observe these people have light within.'

There is irony in the title *Merrily Danced the Quaker's Wife*, for good Quakers regarded dancing as sinful.

Meg Merilees

Meg is a gypsy character who plays an important part in Sir Walter Scott's *Guy Mannering*. She had 'a voice too harsh to be called female, yet too shrill for a man . . . very tall, had a voluminous handkerchief rolled round her head, grizzled hair flowing in elf-locks from beneath it, a long red cloak, and a staff in her hand, headed with a sort of spear point . . . the appearance of this female, and the mixture of frenzy and enthusiasm in her manner, seldom failed to produce the strongest impression upon those whom she addressed'.

Her curse on the Laird of Ellangowan strikes a chord with those who are acquainted with the depopulation of the Highlands — 'This day have ye quenched seven smoking hearths — see if the fire in your ain parlour burn the blyther for that. Ye have riven the thack off seven cottar houses — look if your ain roof-tree stand faster. — Ye may stable your stirks in the shealings at Dern-cleugh — see that the hare does not couch on the hearthstone at Ellangowan. — Ride your ways, Godfrey Bertram — what do ye glower after our folk for? — There's thirty hearts there, that wad hae wanted bread ere ye had wanted sunkets, and spent their life-blood ere ye had scratched your finger. . . . '

As in the tradition of gypsies, Meg was a fortune-teller, a spey-wife, whose clairvoyances are important to Scott's tale, a tale of inheritance re-won in Galloway, on the Borders. Like so many of Scott's most authentic characters, Meg Merilees is drawn, at least substantially, from a real-life model, Jean Gordon, born about the year 1670 at Kirkyetholm, Roxburghshire, and the wife of Patrick Faa, a gypsy chief of that airt. Some of the tales associ-ated with her, her manner and virtues, are characteristic of Meg Merilees. It is said that her granddaughter Madge Gordon also bore strong resemblances, at least in appearance and mannerisms. Thus, Meg Merilees combined the characteristics of both.

Gypsies in Scotland were called 'Egyptians'. By the seven-teenth century, certain families of these frequented certain haunts in the Borders in particular. A similar class of nomad was more numerous in Scotland — the tinker — certain families of which are still to be seen in parts of the West Highlands in the summer months. They have now been eliminated almost entirely by the same pressures which may one day place all wild creatures in zoos. Whether indeed the Border gypsies were of the Romany variety or were simply tinkers in not clear. Perhaps there were strains of both.

Sir Walter Scott writes of the 'gypsies' of Yetholm. A Kelso baillie informed him in 1815 that the colony at Kirk Yetholm amounted to about 109 men, women and children. His remarks on their habits, essentially characteristic of their kind elsewhere in Scotland, are most interesting:

> I have known the colony between forty and fifty years. At my first remembrance of them, they were called the tinklers (tinkers) of Yetholm, from the males being chiefly then employed in mending pots, and other culinary utensils, especially in their peregrinations through the hilly and less populous parts of the country.
>
> Sometimes they were called horners, from their occupation in making and selling horn spoons, called cutties. Now their common appelation is that of muggers, or, what pleases them better, potters. They purchase, at a cheap rate, the cast, or faulty articles, at the dif-ferent manufactories of earthenware, which they carry for sale all over the country; consisting of groups of six, ten, and sometimes

twelve or fourteen persons, male and female, young and old, provided with a horse and cart to transport the pottery, besides shelties
and asses to carry the youngest of the children, and such baggage as
they find necessary.

In the country they sleep in barns and byres, or other out-
houses; and when they cannot find that accommodation, they take
the canvass covering from the pottery cart, and squat below it like a
covey of partridges in the snow.

A few of the colony also employ themselves occasionally in
making besoms, foot bosses, etc., from heath, broom, and bent, and
sell them at Kelso, and the neighbouring towns. After all, their employment can be considered little better than an apology for idleness
and vagrancy.

They are in general great adepts in hunting, shooting, and
fishing; in which last they use the net and spear, as well as the rod;
and often supply themselves with a hearty meal by their dexterity.
They have no notion of their being limited in their field sports,
either to time, place, or mode of destruction.

I do not see that the women are any otherwise employed than
attending the young children, and assisting to sell the pottery when
carried through the country.'

Vagrancy, until comparatively recent times, has been an ever-
present concern for the civil authorities in Scotland, and laws
against 'all vagabonds, called Egyptians' and 'siklike idle persons'
have been passed from time to time through the centuries; but not
all vagrants were gypsies or 'tinklers' or 'horners' or 'cairds', as
the professional nomads were variously called.

James MacPherson, who, at Banff in 1700, 'played a spring
an' danced it roun', aneth the gallows tree', was the son of a Highland gentleman by a gypsy mother. The charge against the fiddler
and his gang was of being 'knowne habit and repute to be Egip-
tians and wagabonds, and keeping the mercats in their ordinarie
manner of thieving and purse cutting , or guilty of the crimes of
thift, masterfull bangstrie and oppressione'.

Burns, at times, allowed himself to rhapsody on the lot of the
vagrant:

> The last o't, the warst o't,
> Is only but to beg.

and pictured vagrant life in recreation at Poosie Nansie's Inn —
'Liberty's a glorious feast!' (*The Jolly Beggars*).

Ae nicht at e'en a merry core
    O randie gangrel bodies
In Poosie Nansie's held the splore,
    To drink their orra duddies
Wi' quaffin', an' laughin',
    They rantit, an' they sang;
Wi' jumpin', an' thumpin',
    The vera girdle rang.

Tinkers' Camp at Moffat (D.O. Hill)

The best-known gypsy name in Scotland is Faa and its most celebrated bearer, Johnny Faa, the gypsy chief whose alleged elopement with Lady Jane, wife of the Sixth Earl of Cassilis in the early seventeenth century, is recorded in an old ballad which Burns claims is the only old song which he could ever trace as belonging to his native county of Ayr. One version of tradition has it, however, that the lady's young lover only disguised himself as a gypsy for the occasion, accompanied by seven or eight accomplices similarly dressed; which sounds altogether more plausible.

However that may be, there are no real gypsies left in Scotland, and authentic tinkers are few. Doubtless many were, and are,

132

living repositories of the old songs and verses of the Scottish countryside, a living remnant of medieval Scotland — Gaberlunzie, 'Egiptian', 'tinkler'. Jeannie Robertson, who gained much celebrity in the 1960's for her singing of Scottish traditional ballads, came of that stock; in her case the nomadic Stewarts and Robertsons of Central Scotland and the North-East.

Earlier in the century, the tinker's essential pursuit was the repairing of pots and pans, supported by some poaching, selling sprigs of heather and singing for a penny. Until World War II, the tinker's horse-drawn caravan or lorry was still a familiar sight on Scotland's roads; pails hanging from the back and a dog padding along, tethered to the axle undernath. The occupants were bronzed and grimy and belonged to a close circle of tinker families interconnected by marriage, which led to the preponderance of certain visible characteristics which in time distinguished them — be it high cheek bones, red or black hair and stocky build. Their modern descendants have old motor trucks and vans instead of pony and trap and frequently someone's cast-off holiday caravan instead of the traditional tent. These make tinkers' camps much less picturesque than those which blended with the countryside in former times. They have fallen on evil days.

Middling, Thank You

This title is obviously the common reply to 'How are you today?' 'Middling' meaning indifferently well.

Midlothian

There are three Lothian counties — East, West and 'Mid'. The Edinburgh Tolbooth was known as the 'Heart' of Midlothian.

Miss Burns' Reel

One cannot be sure, but it seems certain that the Miss Burns honoured by this reel was none other than she who created something of a stir in Edinburgh in the year 1790 when she was brought before the magistrates at the instance of some of her neighbours in Rose Street. She was then but twenty years of age and had not long arrived from her home town, Durham, where on account of the dissolution of her once wealthy father, she had been thrown destitute upon the world. It seems that she had aroused the suspicions of some of the more unctuous members of society regarding the character of her business. Her beauty and stately figure attired in the height of fashion made her a conspicuous figure on the 'Evening Promenades' along Princess Street and attracted too many admiring glances, perhaps, from the ever impressionable Scottish male.

None other than Bailie Creech, Robert Burns' Edinburgh publisher, was on the bench when the lady was arraigned. He passed sentence of banishment 'forth of the city', and confinement for six months in the 'house of correction' and a drumming through the streets if she should return — which testifies to his own susceptibilities. But Miss Burns entered an appeal which was ultimately successful, upon which the douce baillie became the butt of some amusing squibs. What Robert Burns thought of the matter may be found in his letter to Peter Hill, February 2, 1790.

Miss Burns' topical career was brief, for, as was the tragic fate of many a more virtuous beauty of that time, she fell into a premature decline and died — at Roslin, in 1792. Among the works of her poet namesake may be found the following 'Written under the portrait of the celebrated Miss Burns':

> Cease, ye prudes, your envious railing,
>   Lovely Burns has charms — confess;
> True it is, she had one failing —
>   Had a woman ever less!

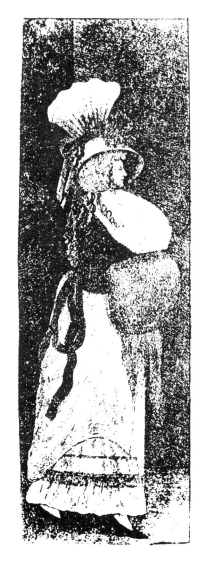

Miss Burns of Edinburgh

Miss Jean Milligan

Jean C. Milligan was a principal founder of the Scottish Country Dance Society but, even more uniquely, she was in many essential ways its creator. She it was who set about collecting the dances and establishing the technique and style of their execution, along with a system of teacher training to ensure the dissemination and perpetuation of what she evolved. She had two careers — one in the first half of her life as a teacher and teacher of teachers of physical education and the other, in the second half, as leader and principal teacher of the Royal Scottish Country Dance Society. In the latter capacity she continued actively to serve until the very end of her life in July 1978 at age 92. Miss Milligan, as she was uniformly styled by all except her closest colleagues and fellow pioneers, was a woman of exceptional force of personality and address. She was capable of inspiring at once love and fear, and even awe, in her auditors and students, while communicating her essential humanity. A benevolent, if sometimes stern leader, she was uncompromising in her idea of her mission, capricious as queens have been known to be and a martinet if the occasion provoked her. She was at heart an Edwardian, a sterling example of the best products of the Glasgow mercantile and professional classes of that age, an age during which Glasgow was proud of its distinction as the Second City of the British Empire and when solid worth and smeddum were qualities highly prized among its sons and daughters. Like most Glaswegians, too, she had more than a trace of Celtic artistry in her veins — be it in music or dance — and a lively, but decorous, sense of humour. Such a combination of qualities — the truly great contrasting dramatically with some very human foibles — endowed her with a unique colour which lent an aura of inspiration to her teaching and eloquence. They were the stuff of legend and, as a legend, Miss Milligan shall be remembered as long as Scotland and her Country Dances endure.

The Montgomeries' Rant

This dance was taken from the Menzies MS., in which it has the distinction of being called a 'Strathspey Reel', the earliest known written record of the term. The R.S.C.D.S., however, has set it to the reel *Lord Eglintoune* composed by the Ayr musician, John Ridell (*c*. 1776). This choice has some relevance as Montgomerie is the family name of the Eglintouns. The alternative tune,

Lady Montgomerie, is, however, a much more satisfactory tune for the dance. It was composed by the Twelfth Earl of Eglintoun and published along with other products of that musical gentleman's talent around 1796.

The Twelfth Earl of Eglintoun was Hugh Montgomerie of Coilsfield, born about 1740; he began his long military career as an ensign at fifteen years of age, served in America and was fourteen years a captain. In 1778, when hostilities broke out with France, he was appointed major in the Argyll or Western Fencibles, and two years later, although a poor public speaker, he successfully stood for Parliament, was returned in 1784 and vacated his seat in 1789 on being appointed Inspector of military roads.

He is the 'soldier Hugh' of Burns' 'Earnest Cry and Prayer to the Scotch Representatives in the House of Commons' :

> Thee, Sodger Hugh, my watchman stented,
> If bardies e'er are represented;
> I ken if that your sword were wanted,
> Ye'd lend your hand:
> But when there's ought to say anent it,
> Ye're at a stand.
>
> (stented — 'vanguard')

'Sodger Hugh' raised or helped raise two other regiments when the need arose in the 1790's, and succeeded his cousin, Archibald, the man honoured by Riddell's tune, to the earldom of Eglintoun just after he was again returned to Parliament in 1796. It was in this same year that some of his compositions — he was an enthusiastic fiddler — were published by Nathaniel Gow. Apart from *Lady Montgomerie's Reel* mentioned here — a really superb tune, it may be said — his *Ayrshire Lasses* and the air for the song *My Gentle Jean* (not very well known), are the most celebrated. The words for the latter were written by Anne Home, the wife of John Hunter, the famous Scots anatomist and assistant to his even more famous brother William. Mrs. Hunter's English lyrics, published in 1802, were much admired in their time; but it is Haydn who has carried her to immortality with his setting of *My Mother bids me bind my Hair*. She died in 1821.

There is an interesting link here with Joanna Baillie, a more gifted poetess who wrote in both the English and Scots tongues (her version of *Woo'd an' married an' a'* is probably her best lyric). Joanna was the daughter of John Hunter's sister and thus Anne Hunter's neice. Brother William, who never married, was the donor of the impressive Hunterian Museum, Glasgow University.

137

To return to 'Sodger Hugh', however, he rebuilt Eglintoun Castle, near Irvine, Ayrshire, and initiated various agricultural and commercial improvements in his locality, dying at eighty years of age in 1819.

The original dance *The Montgomerie's Rant* was recorded in MS. in the time of the Tenth Earl, son of the celebrated Countess Susannah who, with her equally beautiful daughters, was an illustrious patron of the early Edinburgh dance Assembly.

Monymusk

Sir Archibald Grant of Monemusk is one of the great Strathspey tunes, composed by that very original composer in the traditional idioms, Daniel Dow (1732-83), music teacher in Edinburgh.

The name is Gaelic, *moine mus(g)ach*, 'nasty, filthy bog'. Not, perhaps, the most prepossessing of names. The laird of this territory in Aberdeenshire is Grant, Baronet of Monymusk. The Third Baronet, who died in 1796, is doubtless the one honoured by Daniel Dow.

The Moudiewart

A 'moudiewart' (pronounced 'mow' as in 'how'), variously spelt, is a mole. Sometimes this is reduced to 'moudie' and sometimes used of a short dark person with a profusion of hair, and sometimes also as a term of endearment for a child.

The tune, a jig, appears to have been well known in the eighteenth century and first appears in print under the present name in Walsh's *Caledonian Country Dances*. A set of bawdy verses was collected by Burns and included among his *Merry Muses*; but whether these are the original verses, it is not possible to say. There may have been Jacobite connotations in the original song, the 'moudiewart' or mole having a special place in the symbolism of the Jacobites on account of a mole-hill leading to the death of William of Orange. (His horse stumbled on one and threw him).

Burns wrote *O for ane and twenty Tam* to this tune and recommended to Thomson that he set the tune as a Strathspey, saying, 'but if you will get any of your ancienter Scots fiddlers to play you in Strathspey time *The moudiewart* — that is the name of the air — I think it will delight you'. But Thomson set it to *Cold and Raw* instead.

138

Mrs. McLeod of Raasay

The reel tune of this name is published in the fifth Gow Collection with a note — 'An Original Isle of Sky Reel Communicated by Mr. McLeod'. Presumably this is Mr. McLeod of Raasay, an assumption which is supported by the inclusion of *Lord Mauchline's Reel* by 'Mr. McLeod of Rasay' in the same collection.

The name of McLeod of Raasay is permanently associated with the Highland tour of Boswell and Johnson in 1773. The fifth Gow collection was compiled around 1808, thirty-five years later, by which time the Laird of Raasay was James Macleod, son of he who welcomed the famous travellers to his island home.

Few parts of Boswell's *Journal of a tour to the Hebrides* give greater pleasure than the account of life at Raasay. It was early September when the famous pair stepped into the laird's 'coach and six', as he called his six-oared boat, at Broadford in Skye, to sail for Raasay. Dr. Johnson sat high on the stern 'like a magnificent Triton', and it is one of the fascinating things about the great club man that he could adapt himself so well to 'roughing it' in the way he had to do. Even when the wind lashed the sea against the boat as it emerged from the shelter of Scalpa to cross the open sound to its destination, in a way which Boswell 'did not like', Johnson was not perturbed. But when his spurs were dropped overboard in the confusion and hurry, he thought 'there was something wild in letting a pair of spurs be carried into the sea out of a boat'.

It was early September, and the heather would be in bloom, clothing the rocks and hills in quilts of purple and deep blue. But neither writer seemed to take any notice of this.

> We saw before us a beautiful bay,' Boswell writes, 'well defended by a rocky coast; a good family mansion; a fine verdure about it, — with a considerable number of trees; — and beyond it hills and mountains in gradation of wilderness. Our boatmen sung with great spirit. Dr. Johnson observed, that naval musick was very ancient. As we came near the shore, the singing of our rowers was succeeded by that of reapers, who were busy at work, and who seemed to shout as much as to sing, while they worked with a bounding activity. Just as we landed, I observed a cross, or rather the ruins of one, upon a rock, which had to me a pleasing vestige of religion. I perceived a large company coming out from the house. We met them as we walked up. There were Rasay himself; his brother Dr. Macleod; his nephew the Laird of M'Kinnon; the Laird of Macleod of Muiravenside, best known by the name of Sandie Macleod, who was long in exile on account of the part which he took in 1745;

139

and several other persons. We were welcomed upon the green, and conducted into the house, where we were introduced to Lady Rasay, who was surrounded by a numerous family, consisting of three sons and ten daughters. The Laird of Rasay is a sensible, polite, and most hospitable gentleman. I was told that his island of Rasay, and that of Rona, (from which the eldest son of the family has his title,) and a considerable extent of land which he has in Sky, do not altogether yield him a very large revenue: and yet he lives in great splendour; and so far is he from distressing his people, that, in the present rage for emigration, not a man has left his estate.

It was past six o'clock when we arrived. Some excellent brandy was served round immediately, according to the custom of the Highlands, where a dram is generally taken every day. They call it a scalch. On a sideboard was placed for us, who had come off the sea, a substantial dinner, and a variety of wines. Then we had coffee and tea. I observed in the room several elegantly-bound books, and other marks of improved life. Soon afterwards a fidler appeared, and a little ball began. Rasay himself danced with as much spirit as any man, and Malcolm bounded like a roe. Sandie Macleod, who has at times an excessive flow of spirits, and had it now, was, in his days of absconding, known by the name of M'Cruslick, which it seems was the designation of a kind of wild man in the Highlands, something between Proteus and Don Quixotte; and so he was called here. He made much jovial noise. Dr. Johnson was so delighted with this scene, that he said, 'I know not how we shall get away.' It entertained me to observe him sitting by, while we danced, sometimes in deep meditation, — sometimes smiling complacently, — sometimes looking upon Hooke's Roman History, — and sometimes talking a little, amidst the noise of the ball, to Mr. Donald M'Queen, who anxiously gathered knowledge from him. He was pleased with M'Queen, and said to me, 'This is a critical man, sir. There must be great vigour of mind to make him cultivate learning so much in the isle of Sky, where he might do without it. It is wonderful how many of the new publications he has. There must be a snatch of every opportunity.'

Malcolm 'bounding like a roe' was then sixty-two years of age, and had earned a place in history twenty-seven years before, by escorting Prince Charlie from Skye to Raasay and back again during his wanderings after the defeat at Culloden. Boswell and Johnson were extremely interested in talking to all who had known the Prince, including Flora Macdonald. Johnson, particularly, was a Jacobite and regarded it an honour to sleep in a bed once occupied by Charles.

The celebrated Doctor had this to say:

Our reception exceeded our expectations. We found nothing but civility, elegance, and plenty. After the usual refreshments, and the usual conversation, the evening came upon us. The carpet was then rolled off the floor; the musician was called, and the whole company was invited to dance, nor did ever fairies trip with greater alacrity. The general air of festivity which predominated in this place, so far remote from all these regions which the mind has been used to contemplate as the mansions of pleasure, struck the imagination with a delightful surprise, analogous to that which is felt at an unexpected emersion from darkness into light.

When it was time to sup, the dance ceased, and six and thirty persons sat down to two tables in the same room. After supper the ladies sung Erse songs, to which I listened as an English audience to an Italian opera, delighted with the sound of words which I did not understand.

I inquired the subjects of the songs, and was told of one, that it was a love song, and of another, that it was a farewell composed by one of the Islanders that was going, in this epidemical fury of emigration, to seek his fortune in America. What sentiments would rise, on such an occasion, in the heart of one who had not been taught to lament by precedent, I should gladly have known; but the lady, by whom I sat, thought herself not equal to the work of translating.

Mr. Macleod is the proprietor of the islands of Raasay, Rona, and Fladda, and possesses an extensive district in Sky. The estate has not, during four hundred years, gained or lost a single acre. He acknowledges Macleod of Dunvegan as his chief, though his ancestors have formerly disputed the pre-eminence.

One of the old Highland alliances has continued for two hundred years, and is still subsisting between Macleod of Raasay and Macdonald of Sky, in consequence of which, the survivor always inherits the arms of the deceased; a natural memorial of military friendship. At the death of the late Sir James Macdonald, his sword was delivered to the present laird of Raasay.

The family of Raasay consists of the laird, the lady, three sons and ten daughters. For the sons there is a tutor in the house, and the lady is said to be very skilful and diligent in the education of her girls. More gentleness of manners, or a more pleasing appearance of domestick society, is not found in the most polished countries.

Raasay is the only inhabited island in Mr. Macleod's possession. Rona and Fladda afford only pasture for cattle, of which one hundred and sixty winter in Rona, under the superintendence of a solitary herdsman.

The length of Raasay is, by computation, fifteen miles, and the breadth two. These countries have never been measured, and the computation by miles is negligent and arbitrary. We observed in travelling, that the nominal and real distance of places had very little relation to each other. Raasay probably contains near a hundred square miles. It affords not much ground, notwithstanding its extent, either for tillage, or pasture; for it is rough, rocky, and barren. The cattle often perish by falling from the precipices. It is like the other islands, I think, generally naked of shade, but it is naked by neglect; for the laird has an orchard, and very large forest trees grow about his house. Like other hilly countries it has many rivulets. One of the brooks turns a corn-mill, and at least one produces trouts.

All ten daughters of Raasay married well, and their descendants must now be scattered throughout America and the Commonwealth. The last laird of Raasay emigrated one hundred years after the flight of Prince Charlie, leaving but the echoes of an exciting fragment of history for the imaginative ear; the tones of *Mrs. Macleod's Reel* among them.

Mrs. Stewart of Fasnacloich

The family of Stewart of Fasnacloich is a branch of the Stewarts of Appin — other branches are those of Ardshiel, Invernahyle, Auchnacrone and Balachulish. These, along with the Stewarts of Atholl and Balquhidder, comprise the Highland clan Stewart. The Atholl Stewarts, interestingly enough, are almost entirely descended from the five illegitimate sons of Sir Alexander Stewart, the

Earl of Buchan, best known as the *Wolf of Badenoch*, a very nasty man who perpetuated his memory by destroying Elgin Cathedral.

The male progenitor of all the Stewarts was an Anglo Norman, Walter, who was appointed hereditary high steward of the household of King David I (1124-1153) of Scotland. Walter was granted the lands of Renfrew, Paisley, Pollock, Cathcart and surroundings and in due course the surname Stewart was applied to the family. His descendant, the sixth high steward, also named Walter, commanded with Douglas the left wing of the Scots army at Bannockburn, and it is to this doughty warrior that King Robert (Bruce) gave his daughter Marjory in marriage and thus laid the foundation of the royal house of Stewart. The later royal Stewarts adopted Stuart, the French spelling of their name.

The Mrs. Stewart of Fasnacloich commemorated by the Country Dance so named, initiated the movement which reached fruition in the Royal Scottish Country Dance Society. She interested Jean C. Milligan, then head teacher of Physical Education at the Jordanhill Teachers' Training College, Glasgow, in her proposal to rescue from oblivion the Scottish Country Dances she had known and enjoyed as a girl and perhaps to promote their re-acceptance into Scottish social life. The rest is history well known to devotees of Scottish Country Dancing. A meeting of interested people was called in Glasgow in the winter of 1923 and the Scottish Country Dance Society was there inaugurated.

Mrs. Stewart died at her home in South Africa, whence she had emigrated, in October 1968 and a memorial plaque is to be seen in the old parish church at Kilmartin, Argyll.

Muirland Willie

This is the title of a popular seventeenth century song. The tune is a jig of rare beauty which has several well-known relatives such as the tune of the Northumbrian *Where have you been all the day?* It is also a relative of *Greensleeves* and has at least one more recent derivative, *Reel of Mey*. Fortunately, the R.S.C.D.S. has published the Country Dance *Muirland Willie* with its name tune.

The ballad, Muirland Willie, was regarded as very old in the eighteenth century. It tells a humorous tale of border "reiving".

My Love, she's but a lassie yet

This well-known tune first appears in Bremner's *Collection* (1757) entitled *Miss Farquharson's Reel* and Stenhouse writes that he saw a manuscript copy of it, entitled *Lady Badinscoth's Reel*. It is of the character of a Scottish Measure, but a Strathspey version exists (see Athol *Collection*) under the title *Gordons hae the Girdin' o't*. Burns may have taken the tune, or its name, from Aird's *Airs* 1782, ii, n.I, where it first appears in print as *My love she's but a lassie yet*, and as was his practice wrote verses developed from the theme of the title — all indeed of this song, as it appears in the *Museum*, except the last four lines:

My love, she's but a lassie yet,
My love, she's but a lassie yet;
  We'll let her stand a year or twa,
She'll no be hauf sae saucy yet;
I rue the day I sought her, O!
I rue the day I sought her, O!
  Wha gets her needna say he's woo'd,
But he may say he's bought her, O!

Come draw a drap o' the best o't yet,
Come draw a drap o' the best o't yet;
  Gae seek for pleasure whar ye will,
But here I never miss'd it yet.
We're a' dry wi' drinkin' o't,
We're a' dry wi' drinkin' o't;
  The minister kiss'd the fiddler's wife —
He couldna preach for thinkin' o't.

My only Jo and Dearie, O

A song of this name was sung in a late eighteenth century pantomime, *Harlequin Highlander*, produced at the Edinburgh Circus and heard there by Thomas Oliver, an Edinburgh printer who was so captivated by the melody that he later asked his friend Richard Gall to write an appropriate set of verses to it, which he did, ending each verse with the title of the tune. This song is sometimes named after its first line — 'Thy Cheek is o' the Rose's Hue'.

Gall, it may be said, died in 1801 at the early age of twenty-five. His poetical works were not published until 1819. The composer of the tune, a Scottish Measure, is unknown.

Thomas Wilson, the eminent London dancing master, published, as was his practice, three alternative sets of Country Dance figures to the tune, the best of which was taken by the R.S.C.D.S. But the Society, while retaining the title, dropped the tune in favour of a Strathspey — *Miss Jean Stewart*, composed and first published by the great William Marshall (the Society attributes the source to Morrison's *Collection*). Thus, again, we have only the title to relate the dance to the song.

The word 'Jo' is short for 'joy', the Scots pronunciation sounding the 'o' as in joe.

The Netherbow has Vanished

The Netherbow, a neck in the lower end of the High Street of Edinburgh, has not vanished, but the great 'port' or city gate which once formed (just below John Knox's house) a handsome and historic barrier to access from the Holyrood side of the city, was demolished in 1764. As an ornament and relic of historical interest, its demise is to be regretted, and indeed but twenty-seven years earlier, the officials of Edinburgh had effectively resisted an attempt by the House of Lords to have the Netherbow Port razed to the ground because of an incident of civil disorder known as the Porteous Riots, which is described earlier in this book under *Madge Wildfire*.

When the delegation returned from London on that occasion, the citizens of Edinburgh lined their route into the city. Bells rang and the crowds cheered, and the gates of the Netherbow Port, which had been unhooked, were re-hung with acclaim. It was, after all, a victory for Scotland. But, in 1764, the port was voluntarily and unceremoniously dismantled for ever.

It had the appearance of a two-storey crenelated stone building with a broad passage running right through it, and a smaller passage, for pedestrian traffic, to one side. Two round towers flanked the gate on the outer face and a handsome square clock-tower and spire was superimposed.

Its Latin inscription ran:

Watch towers and thund'ring walls vain fences prove
No guards to monarchs like their people's love.

JACOBUS VI. REX, ANNA REGINA, 1606

This structure replaced a previous port which had become derelict, in 1606; but nevertheless, it too had presided over some historic comings and goings. The last of these occurred in September 1745 when Prince Charles' small, orderly and enthusiastic band approached the city. A deputation of the magistrates set out to treat with the rebels and returned after dark, about ten at night, with a letter from Charles demanding peaceable admittance. A little later in the night, a detachment of 900 men under Lochiel, Ardsheil and Keppoch approached the vicinity of the Netherbow Port with the intention of forcing entry.

As luck would have it, the coach which had returned the magistrates was then being driven back out of the town to the stables near Holyrood. Halting at the port, the driver is reported to have called to the sentry 'Open the port, for I behove to get out.'

The Netherbow Port, Old Edinburgh

146

'You cannot,' replied the sentry, 'without an order from the Provost.' The under-keeper of the port intervened, however, to state that he had orders to let the coach pass; but when the ponderous gate was pulled back, a Highlander — no less than the worthy Lochiel himself — leapt out of the dark and disarmed the sentry — the town was taken!

What a stirring, what excitement, the pipes echoed round the closes and gables, and worthy burgesses startled from their beds crowded to the windows to see their colourful countrymen from the West Highlands, colours flying, swords drawn, march towards the Castle — what was it the pipes were playing?

> We'll awa tae Shirramuir,
> And haud the Whigs in order.

An allusion to the Battle of Sherrifmuir of the previous rebellion in 1715.

It was a peaceful, bloodless occupation. The City guards were disarmed and Highland pickets were placed at the eight ports. Which brings us to the subject of the Ports of Edinburgh. Perhaps we would be inclined to say the 'gates' of Edinburgh, but the word 'port' was used by the people of the town; a 'gate' or 'gait' was a roadway. They would never have said the 'Netherbow gate'.

Edinburgh in the fifteenth century comprised little more than the castle on the rock and some houses of the aristocracy and lesser burgesses scattered before it. This cluster was encircled by a defensive wall in 1450, the North flank was protected by the Nor' Loch, which is now converted into a railway track, and Princes Street Gardens. But when the tragic news of the destruction of the flower of Scotland's manhood at Flodden (1512) arrived, all resources were mobilized to prepare the defence of the city, and a new wall was hastily constructed to embrace the enlarged town.

There were then six ports, starting with the port nearest the castle — the West Port, The Vennel, the Society Port, the Potterrow Port, the Cowgate Port and the Netherbow Port. The word 'nether' means 'lower', here used to distinguish the 'lower' bow from the 'upper' or west bow. Two other ports were added later — the New Port and the Bristo Port. Little trace of the wall remains and the ports survive only in name.

147

Nineteenth of December

On this date, 1745, Prince Charlie's Highlanders re-grouped in Carlisle on their retreat North after their advance to within 127 miles of London.

None so Pretty

A pink wild flower familiar in the South of England.

The Oxton Reel

Oxton is a village in Lauderdale, a district south of Edinburgh. The dance is a sixsome reel popular in that region within living memory. Another sixsome was favoured in the nearby town of Lauder and called *The Lauder Reel*. This has not been published by the R.S.C.D.S. These reels, of course, are not Country Dances.

Petronella

Variously spelled *Petronnelle, Paternally, Paternella* ('Little Peter'). The tune is a hornpipe of the rhythmical character of a Scottish Measure, but the melody is not Scottish in character. This Country Dance and its tune, has been popular in Scotland from about the early nineteenth century well into the present. It was therefore among the first dances collected by the R.S.C.D.S.

Push about the Jorum

The word 'jorum' is of Anglo-Saxon origin, and was used of a large pot, bowl or jug. It was used in England, especially Northumberland, in the eighteenth century and is blood relative to the word 'jordan' or Chaucer's 'jordane'. Clearly here it is used of a large jug of ale. The tune of this name is English, and indeed was composed in 1770 for a song in the opera *The Golden Pippin*. Campbell included it as *The Jorum* in his collection of Reels eight

148

years later, and Aird published it under its present name in 1782. It is a good marching tune and Burns liked it sufficiently to use it as the vehicle of his patriotic song *The Dumfries Volunteers*. Two companies of volunteers were raised in Dumfries when the French Convention menaced the country in the early part of 1795. There is something ironical in the supporter of the principles of the French and American revolutions, hastening to join the local volunteers and shouldering pike or gun in weekly drills to the great detriment of his failing health. On top of this, he, being an exciseman, was officially censured for his revolutionary views, and his last days were filled with anxiety as his tailor, viewing with apprehension the probable decease of the client, threatened to start proceedings for recovery of the cost of the 'volunteer' uniform he had made for him. Burns, his low state of health and expectation of death enlarging all his fears, wrote to his father's brother in Montrose for help to appease the irate tailor and save him from the debtor's prison. William Burness — he continued to use the old spelling of his name — forwarded the necessary help without question and thus became another of his family deserving of his country's honour.

This story is well known to students of Robert Burns and serves as a kind of sad 'owercome' of the patriotic song which Burns wrote for the gallant volunteers to the tune of *Push about the Jorum*:

Does haughty Gaul invasion threat?

Miss Catley, a singer much in vogue in the late eighteenth century, was celebrated for the song *Push about the Jorum* in the part of Juno in *Midas*. This she sang with a mug in her hand. (Cf. Henry Mackenzie, *Anecdotes and Egotisms*, p.210.)

When bickerings hot
To high words got
Break out at Janicorum,
The golden rule
The flame to cool
Is — push about the Jorum
With Can or Jug —
Who can lug,
Or shew me that glib speaker
Who her red rag
In wrath can wag
When her mouth's full of liquor.

149

Queen's Welcome

This dance was collected in Perthshire and Peebleshire; where it originated or the particular occasion which inspired it is not known. There is no tune of the same name associated with the dance, hence it belongs to that category of Country Dance in which the name is associated with the figures rather than the tune. The tunes specified for it by the R.S.C.D.S. are the reels *Lochearn* and *Donald's awa to the War*, comparatively recent pipe tunes.

The queen referred to here is undoubtedly Queen Victoria. Her passion for the Highlands is well known and recorded in her own words in her published diaries. She made several tours through Perthshire and adjacent counties and one or two in the Borders during her long reign, both before and after the death of Albert. Perhaps the most elaborate welcome arranged for her was that by Lord Breadalbane at Taymouth in 1842 when all his Highlanders were arrayed in the national dress, lining the avenues, carrying torches, dancing reels and Gille Callum to the pipes in a superbly staged setting. Twenty-four years later, the Queen recalled this on returning to the scene: 'I gazed, not without deep inward emotion, on the scene of our reception, twenty-four years ago, by dear Lord Breadalbane in a princely style, not to be equalled for grandeur and poetic effect!'

Perhaps this was the occasion inspiring our dance; it would be very appropriate if it were so. An interesting personal note may have a place here. My late elderly friend Jamie MacKellar, a true Gael, of Tayvallich, Knapdale, told me how he had picked up the Country Dance *The Queen's Welcome* and the *Eightsome Reel* in Lochgilphead nearby, and introduced them to the Loch Sween region in the early years of the present century.

Rachel Rae

Rachel Rae was the dedicatee of a tune of that name by Joseph Lowe, the fiddler and dancing master of the first half of the nineteenth century, who, for a time embraced Balmoral and vicinity in his itinerary.

Red House or *Where will bonnie Annie lie?*

The tune apparently known in England as the *Red House*, and in Scotland, *Where will our gudeman lie?* appears, according to James Dick, in a Northumberland MS. dated 1694, as *Rood house rant*. It also appears in the edition of Playford's Dancing Master of the next year as *Red House*. Alan Ramsay took it up and set new verses to it beginning 'Where wad bonny Annie ly?' which were published in 1724. About fifty years later, Burns used the tune for another theme, 'O, wha my baby-clouts will buy?', which, as he tells us, he sent 'to a young girl, a very particular acquaintance of mine, who was at that time under a cloud'.

The next event in the history of this tune occurred around 1840, when the song *D'ye ken John Peel* was composed by J.P. Groves, a gentleman in Westmorland, and set to a modification of its second measure.

The Country Dance *Red House* was taken by the R.S.C.D.S. from Walsh's *Caledonian country dances* (1750), where it is specifically designated in the text as a 'Scotch country dance'. A few other dances in the same collection are so designated yet have titles which are most un-Scottish!

Examples of the principal settings of the tune, as a Scottish Measure, may be of interest:

Oldest Set:

O whar'll our gudeman lie,
gudeman lie, gudeman lie,
O whar'll our gudeman lie,
till he shute o'er the simmer?
Up amang the hen-bawks,
the hen bawks, the hen bawks,
Up amang the hen-bawks,
amang the rotten timmer.

Ramsay's (1st verse):

O where wad bonie Annie ly,
Alone nae mair ye mauna ly;
Wad ye a goodman try,
Is that the thing ye're lacking.
O can a lass sae young as I,
Venture on the bridal tye.
Syne down with a goodman ly
I'm flee'd he'd keep me wauking.

Burns:

O wha my baby-clouts will buy?
Wha will tent me when I cry?
Wha will kiss me where I lie?
The rantin dog the daddie o't.
Wha will own he did the faut?
Wha will buy the groanin maut?
Wha will tell me how to ca't?
The rantin dog the daddie o't.

When I mount the creepie-chair,
Wha will set beside me there?
Gie me Rob, I'll seek nae mair, —
The rantin dog the daddie o't.
Wha will crack to me my lane?
Wha will mak me fidgin fain?
Wha will kiss me o'er again? —
The rantin dog, the daddie o't.

I have given Burns in full because it is a good example of his deft grasp of the traditional idiom. It also casts an interesting light on the poet's characteristic attitude to fatherhood — 'wha will own he did the faut? — The rantin dog the daddie o't'.

The 'groaning maut (malt)' was the name given to the ale customarily brewed on the occasion of a birth and the 'creepie-chair' is the penance stool on which such offenders of the moral law were obliged to stand 'sabbathly, induring the kirk session 's will'.

Reel of the 51st Division

The 51st Highland Division played a conspicuous part in covering the evacuation of the British Expeditionary Force through Dunkirk in 1940, during World War II. Partly to execute this task and partly to encourage the French, the division was sacrificed in a stand at St. Valery and Calais. It was later reconstituted and was prominent in the North African desert campaign and in the invasion of Europe in 1943.

Meantime, those who were taken prisoner at St. Valery were incarcerated in German prison camps. At one of these, Laufen, three officers (Peter Oliver, Jimmy Atkinson and Harris Hunter) devised a Country Dance which they called the *Laufen Reel*. Despite the fact that the instructions resembled a code, the dance was sent home to Mrs. Hunter who was an enthusiastic country dancer in Perth. On her suggestion the name of the dance was changed to *The St. Valery Reel*, and it was by this title that the dance first became well known. When, in 1945, the R.S.C.D.S. published the dance in the 'Victory' Book, the title *Reel of the 51st Division* was adopted. St. Valery, after all, did not convey happy memories for the 51st Division. The opening figure, too, was modified from dancing couple casting off to meet below fourth couple, to meeting below third couple. This made it conform to established practice for a three-couple dance and a four-couple set. The tune selected, *The Drunken Piper*, is a popular pipe reel, much favoured by military pipe bands and composed by Alex. McLeod (*c*. 1880).

This was the first contemporary Country Dance to be published by the R.S.C.D.S. and it received much publicity and attention in its time from the circumstances of its composition.

152

The Reel of Tulloch (or Reel o' Thulichan or Hoolichan)

The ancient village of Tulloch lies near the Pass of Ballater leading into that magnificent Highland region known as the Braes of Mar. There is a tradition that some time in the seventeenth century, on a very stormy Sunday morning, a number of the congregation of the auld kirk of Tulloch arrived for the service only to find that the minister, not expecting his parishioners to venture out in such weather, had remained at home. The people stamped their feet and clapped their hands to raise a little warmth, then someone produced some ale — so it is said — and a quartet of the young ones started to dance. A musician seems to have been at hand and with his help the special reel was improvised which ever after bore the name *Reel of Tulloch*.

The disturbing thing about this story is that others exist, although the theme is similar. Whatever its origin, there is no mention of the dance *Reel of Tulloch* prior to the nineteenth century in any of the allusions to Scottish dance, which could mean, of course, that it was then enjoyed in a very restricted local circle. The tune, certainly, is old; it is included in the Drummond Castle MS. (1734), and there is no denying that this is the tune peculiarly belonging to the dance. It seems most likely that the tune and the dance were improvised together. The Reel o' Tulloch was demonstrated 'with admirably characteristic spirit' by the Marquis of Abercorn, the Hon. Fox Maule, Cluny Macpherson and Davidson of Tulloch, at the ball given by the Marquis of Breadalbane on the occasion of Queen Victoria's celebrated visit to Taymouth Castle in 1842. 'The Queen,' commented the dancing master, Joseph Lowe, 'seemed quite elated during the performance of this ancient Reel, and expressed herself much delighted and astonished at the lively execution displayed by the dancers.' Hence the occasional reference to this reel in the nineteenth century as the Breadalbane Ball Reel.

153

The Rock and the Wee Pickle Tow

The 'rock' — spinning wheel, and the 'wee pickle' — small piece, of 'tow' — prepared flax. The tune appears in John Playford's *Musick's Hand-Maid* (1678) as *A Scottish March* and a set of somewhat coarse verses were current before Alex. Ross, schoolmaster and poet of Lochlee, Forfarshire, wrote his own better known words which are to be found in Herd.

In the South-West of Scotland, and particularly in Ayrshire, it seems to have been the custom for housewives or housemaids to convene, perhaps in one another's house or, perhaps, as in Highland villages, in one particular house recognized as a common rendezvous, taking their spinning wheels — 'rocks' — along with them. These meetings were called 'rockings meets' or simply 'rocks' or 'rockins'. When cottage spinning became a thing of the past, the social meeting in the house of a neighbour was still called a 'rock' and so when one neighbour said to another — 'I am coming over with my *rock*', he meant simply that he intended to visit for the evening. (*Stat. Acct. of Scotland, VII*, Muirkirk, pp.612-13.)

Rory O'More

The name of this jig comes from a ballad composed by the Irishman, Samuel Lover (1797-1868), in 1826 which he later expanded into a popular romance in 1837.

Round About Hullochan

This is a name for a round-the-room version of the *Reel of Tulloch* which was a particular favourite in the Borders in the late nineteenth century.

St. Andrew's Day

Andrew, disciple of Jesus Christ, is believed to have travelled as a missionary through the Celtic community of Asiatic and European Scythia thence through Thrace, Macedonia and Epirus into Achaia where, in the city of Patra, he suffered martyrdom by crucifixion, at the hands of the Romans, in 70 A.D. He was fastened by cords to a diagonal cross and left to endure a lingering death by starvation and thirst.

The body of St. Andrew was exhumed in the fourth century by the Emperor Constantine and removed to Constantinople. Thirty years after Constantine's death in 368 A.D., a pious Greek monk, named Regulus or Rule, is said to have conveyed St. Andrew's remains to Scotland and deposited them on the coast of Fife where he built a church and where, in medieval times, was raised a great cathedral in the midst of a town named after the saint. St. Andrew was henceforth regarded as the patron saint of Scotland and his cross, white on a dark blue background, serves as the flag of Scotland. St. Andrew's day is November 30.

The celebration of St. Andrew's day was discontinued in Scotland after the Reformation; but, curiously enough, it has been assiduously observed by Scottish emigrants abroad, particularly by the friendly societies named after the saint which were founded in the nineteenth century in foreign parts to help indigent Scottish emigrants.

Saw ye my wee Thing

This was another name for the verses entitled *Mary of Castle Cary*, written by Hector Macneill and first published in 1791. It was later set to the tune, *Bonnie Dundee*, in which form it was surprisingly popular, well into the nineteenth century, although it is hardly great art and not a little ridiculous in places. Macneill wrote a few successful love songs of the kind and it is curious that, in most of them, the lovers are a young lass and a much older man or vice versa.

> Saw ye my wee thing? Saw ye my ain thing?
> Saw ye my true love down by yon lea?
> Cross'd she the meadow yestreen at the gloaming?
> Sought she the burnie whar flow'rs the haw tree?
> Her hair it is lint-white, her skin it is milk-white;
> Dark is the blue o' her saft rolling e'e!
> Red red her lips, and sweeter than roses;
> Whar could my wee thing wander frae me?

Scottish Reform

Henry Cockburn, referring to the period around 1800 in Scotland, writes:

> Everything rang, and was connected with the Revolution in France; which, for above twenty years, was the all in all. Everything, literally everything, was soaked in this one event.
> Yet, we had wonderfully few proper Jacobins; that is, persons who seriously wished to introduce a republic into this country, on the French precedent.

Anyone, however, who was known to entertain sympathies for the French Revolutionary cause, or who had a taste for reform, was liable to be *called* a Jacobin. But, to quote Cockburn again (*Memorials of his Times*, Edinburgh.):

> If Scotch Jacobinism did not exist, Scotch Toryism did, and with a vengeance. This party engrossed almost the whole wealth, and rank, and public office, of the country, and at least three-fourths of the population. They could have afforded, therefore, to be just and well-tempered. But this, as it appeared to them, would have endangered their supremacy. Hence the great Tory object was to abuse everybody but themselves, and in particular to ascribe a thirst for bloodshed and anarchy, not merely to their avowed public opponents, but to the whole body of the people.
> With the people suppressed and the Whigs powerless, Government was the master of nearly every individual in Scotland, but especially in Edinburgh, which was the chief seat of its influence. The pulpit, the bench, the bar, the colleges, the parliamentary electors, the press, the magistracy, the local institutions, were so completely at the service of the party in power, that the idea of independence, besides being monstrous and absurd, was suppressed by a feeling of conscious ingratitude. Henry Dundas, an Edinburgh man, and well calculated by talent and manner to make despotism popular, was the absolute dictator of Scotland, and had the means of rewarding submission and of extinguishing opposition beyond what were ever exercised in modern times by one person in any portion of the empire.

From the Treaty of Union with England, 1707, until 1832, the forty alleged representatives of Scotland, it has been said, represented nobody but 'the great lord, the drunken laird, and the drunkener baillie'. (Meikle: *Scotland and the French Revolution*, Edinburgh, 1912.) No man unable to prove himself an owner of an 'assured income' could stand for parliament, but in any case, as

156

Cockburn remarks, the Westminster Government was, through its agents, master of nearly every individual in Scotland. There were no free institutions.

Scottish engineers and scientists played no small part in the evolution of the new industrial society, a society which gave rise to a new class of merchant barons and capitalists. This class, the 'middle class', looked somewhat sourly on the abuse of their taxes and their lack of representation, and it is from this — as well as from the democratic views of numerous young professional people — that the Scottish reform movement sprang. The remedy, they thought, lay in shorter Parliaments and wider representation.

The French and American revolutions were violent expressions of the same sort of discontent with a similar tyranny. It is understandable that the rebels against arbitrary authority in Scotland should look with zealous sympathy on the French revolutionaries, and that the Government should regard them with like apprehension.

Add to the corruption of Scottish representation and rule the destruction of the home industries by the machine, the removal of the Highland peasantry from the land of their forefathers and the iniquity of the factory system at its crudest, and we can have no difficulty in understanding the fascination of the achievements of the American colonists and the inspiration of the fall of the Bastille extending down into the 'lower orders' — as craftsmen and shopkeepers, etc., were regarded even by their middle-class employers.

Prominent among those who strove to organize for reform was Thomas Muir, son of the landed proprietor of Huntershill, near Glasgow, and an advocate by profession. On October 30, 1792, incidentally the year of a harvest failure, we find him organizing a meeting in the Star Hotel, Glasgow, to form a branch of the 'Friends of the People Society' of which the objective was nothing more demanding than 'equal political representation and shorter parliaments'. A proliferation of such societies now occurred, and all were united in their conception of the House of Commons, as 'a vile junta of aristocrats', as it was expressed in a letter addressed to Thomas Muir which led to his arrest on a charge of sedition in 1793.

The excesses of the French revolutionaries sobered many of the more moderate Whigs and thoroughly alarmed the aristocracy. Paine's *Rights of Man* was suppressed, but very ineffectually, even being distributed in a Gaelic version, in the Highlands. There seemed little opportunity of effecting reform without force, and the aristocratic rulers had no intention of allowing scope for any alternative. So the leaders of the reform movement had to be removed, and its organization crushed.

Scotland had the right man on the bench for that job — Robert McQueen, Lord Braxfield, Scotland's 'hanging judge'. He emerges from the pages of history as a coarse and brutal tyrant, an image which obscures whatever merits he had in the way of natural ability and practical sense. There have been some attempts to whitewash him (Roughhead: *The Real Braxfield, Juridical Rev.*, May 1914 and March 1922.) and to blame Cockburn's *Memorials* for his ill-repute; but the record is there for all to read and the legend is surely too strong to be refuted.

Cockburn describes him thus: 'strong built and dark with rough eyebrows, powerful eyes, threatening lips, and a low growling voice, he was like a formidable blacksmith. His accent and his dialect were exaggerated Scotch, his language, like his thoughts, short, strong and conclusive.'

In the political trials of 1793-4, he obviously believed that the temper of the times and the threat to established order personified by the brave and able men brought before him, demanded his utmost severity. This, however, he did not restrain to purely judicial channels, but allowed to colour his casual remarks and conduct on the bench. The most distinguished of his victims were — Muir, Palmer, Skirving, Margarot and Gerrold — all sentenced to transporation for fourteen years.

But it is too much to say they were Braxfield's victims alone, Lords Henderland, Eskgrove and Swinton shared the bench as Justiciary Judges, and they had a packed jury and the State behind them.

Several defence witnesses, too, were committed to prison on the most frivolous pretexts.

When the sordid details of these disgraceful trials reached London, Fox, leader of the Whig opposition, and several others moved to have the proceedings quashed. Sheridan declared 'that such a sentence in Scotland, if pronounced in England, would be enough to rouse the people of England to arms'. Nevertheless, both houses overwhelmingly rejected the motion for clemency.

Muir, Palmer, Skirving and Margarot were now manacled and chained in the hulks, ready to be shipped in some equally loathsome convict ship to Australia. Knowing that if they survived the heat of the tropics in such circumstances and in these fetid surroundings, they would count themselves fortunate. They arrived safely in Sydney, after a punishing voyage, in 1794.

The shocking story of the Scottish Reform trial came to the attention of George Washington in America. Now began another fantastic episode in the career of Thomas Muir, which makes fact stranger than fiction. Washington ordered a ship, the *Otter*, to be fitted out in New York for the purpose of effecting a rescue of the condemned men. This ship reached Sydney, February 1796, and after a few days, left with Thomas Muir aboard. Margarot declined to leave and the other two were too seriously ill to consider it. The news of Muir's escape reached Scotland, and none, we can imagine, more earnestly rejoiced than his elderly parents who had barely been able to see their son before he was taken away.

But the *Otter* never reached the United States, nor did Muir, for the ship ran into a hurricane and was cast up on rocks near Nootka Sound, and broken asunder by the waves. All on board perished except — and it is difficult to surpass this — Thomas Muir and two others. They wandered for a time on a deserted shore then were separated from each other.

Not long after, Muir ran into a tribe of Indians who, to his relief and mystification, we may imagine, treated him with every honour and distinction. After some weeks in this predicament, he managed to escape, travelling for many weeks without meeting a soul and ultimately reaching Panama. There he obtained an interview with the Spanish Governor, who was moved by Muir's strange story to help him contact an American vessel to take him to New York. Escorted by a party of Spaniards, Muir was conducted across the Isthmus to Vera Cruz but on no American ship appearing, he was sent on to Havana. Now fate took another perverse twist. For some unknown reason, perhaps because there was no immediate alternative, the Governor of Havana placed him aboard one of two frigates then setting out with a rich cargo for Cadiz.

Unfortunately, at that time, Britain was at war with France and Spain, and Admiral Jervis was blockading Cadiz with his squadron. The two Spanish frigates heaving into sight were an easy prey, and after a short and punishing fight were forced to strike their colours. But, alas, Thomas Muir lay in a pool of blood, to all appearances mortally wounded, one side of his face grievously torn by a ball.

The officer who led the boarding party gave orders for the dead to be thrown overboard, loaded with lead bullets. On turning over Muir's body, he came across the bible which Muir had been given by his parents on his departure and which he had carried with him through all his tribulations. The officer read the name 'Thomas Muir', and — again the fact defies fiction — this officer was none other than a friend and companion of Muir's days at Glasgow College!

Finding that Muir was still alive, he bound up his wounds and had him conveyed ashore by a pinnace carrying a flag of truce. He must have reported that Muir was one of the dead, for a letter containing this news was published in the *Edinburgh Advertiser*, June 1797.

Muir, however, survived his wounds for a time, but was held prisoner by the Spaniards until the French Directory intervened. In September 1797, the French Government applied to the Spanish Government to permit Muir's safe conduct to France and offered Muir French citizenship. He arrived at Bordeaux in the following December, and was feted there at a splendid banquet attended by the American Consul.

He reached Paris, February 4, 1798, in a very weak condition, deeply grateful to the French for their generosity towards him, and honoured by the solicitous attentions of many members of the Government. But sad to relate, he fell a victim to his wounds in the September of that year.

This was not the end of the story of Scottish Reform, but unfortunately there is no space here to relate in full the struggles of these times. In 1820, however, discontent had reached the stage of pikes and weapons being manufactured and stored in preparation for an uprising which Government *agents provocateurs* and informants precipitated so that its leaders could be hanged. There were Government spies who framed cases against innocent people, and there were harrowing martyrdoms in the cause — the cause, not of dictatorship of the proletariat, but of a slightly wider representation in parliament to modify the tyranny of a landed aristocracy.

Scotland did not suffer alone, but it suffered most, and when the populace gathered at the Glasgow Tontine Inn to receive the news of the enactment of the Great Reform Bill of 1832, coming in by the London stage, they were marking an important milestone in the history of democracy and the cause of Scottish Reform.

Seann Triubhas Willichan

Pronounced 'Shan trews Willichan'. 'Willie's old trousers' — the name of an old Highland step-dance or character 'jig'. The tune, familiar in eighteenth century Scottish dancing schools, is a Scottish Measure and a set of 'De'il Stick the Minister', as is 'This is no my Ain Hoose' and some others. It lends itself readily to Strathspey treatment. Curiously, it is no longer used for the

160

well-known character solo dance, now best known simply as *Seann Triubhas*, having been replaced for that duty by 'Whisle o'er the lave o't', at least since about the latter half of the nineteenth century. The Country Dance published by the R.S.C.D.S. is attributed to Thomas Wilson's *Companion to the Ballroom*; but, as is so often the case with the Society's reconstructions, and often necessarily so, it is a very free adaption indeed. In addition, the name tune has been jettisoned in favour of an andante Scottish hornpipe air entitled 'My Dearie'. The dance is to be executed in Strathspey style. Only the title really remains, and it is a pity thus to preclude the use of the illustrious old tune in association with a country dance bearing its name.

She's Ower Young to Marry Yet

This title should read 'I'm' instead of 'She's'. Slightly different sets of the tune are included in several eighteenth century collections and Burns wrote verses for it, retaining the original chorus which was old. G.F. Graham, however, did not think that Burns had gone far enough to 'mitigate' the 'rude old words'.

> I am my mammy's ae bairn,
>   Wi' unco folk I weary sir,
> And lying in a man's bed,
>   I'm fley'd it mak me eerie sir.
>
> Chorus:
> I'm o'er young, I'm o'er young,
> I'm o'er young tae marry yet!
> I'm o'er young, 'twad be a sin
> To tak me frae my mammy yet.

A specimen of the 'rude old words' has come down to us!

> My minnie coft me a new gown,
> The Kirk maun hae the gracing o't,
> Were I to lie with you kind sir,
> I'm fear'd ye'd spoil the lacing o't.

The dance is taken from Thomson, 1751.

161

Sodger Laddie

The tune of this name first appears in early MSS. as *Northland Ladie* before it was published as *Sodger Laddie* by Watt and Walsh (1731) and in the *Orpheus Caledonius* (1733). It was very popular in eighteenth century Scotland, and Burns made a song to it for inclusion in his cantata *The Jolly Beggars:*

> I once was a maid tho' I cannot tell when,
> And still my delight is in proper young men;
> Some one of a troop of dragoons was my dadie;
> No wonder I'm fond of a sodger laddie.
>   etc. etc.

Ramsay wrote less ribald verses about half a century earlier, developed from an old verse current in his time:

> My sodger laddie is over the sea
> And he'll bring gold and money to me;
> And when he comes home he'll make me a Lady,
> My blessings gang wi' my sodger laddie.

This shows how 'Sailor Laddie' became yet another title for the tune.

The Sow's Tail

The proper title is *The Sow's tail to Geordie* — from a Jacobite song of the early eighteenth century which was a scurrilous lampoon of George I and his mistress, Madame Kilmansegge, whom he brought with him, along with the rest of his belongings, from Hanover. The complete song is to be found in Hogg's *Jacobite Relics*. Madame Kilmansegge, or the Countess of Darlington as she became, was called 'The Elephant' in England; a nickname suggested by her ample proportions. The Scots Jacobites, however, were not so fastidious and called her 'The Sow'. Here are some verses from the song:

It's Geordie's now come hereabout,
O wae light on his ugly snout!
A pawky sow has found him out,
    And turned her tail to Geordie.

It's Geordie he gat up to dance,
And wi' the sow to take a prance,
And aye she gart her hurdies flaunce,   Chorus:
    And turned her tail to Geordie.   The sow's tail is till him yet,
                                      A sow's birse will kill him yet,
                                      The sow's tail is till him yet,
It's Geordie he sat down to dine,   The sow's tail to Geordie.
And who came in but Madam Swine?
'Grumph! Grumph!' quo' she, 'I've come in time,
    I'll set and dine wi' Geordie.'

It's Geordie he lay down to die;
The sow was there as weel as he:
'Umph! Umph!' quo' she, 'he's no for me,'
    And turned her tail to Geordie.

The tune is a 'mild' Scottish Measure, and is published in McGlashan's *Collection*. Burns liked it and wrote a dialogue duet to it for Thomson entitled 'O Philly, happy be that day'.

The Gows published the tune in Strathspey style with variations 'for the Piano Forte, Violin &c' in their *Second Collection* (1803), and this is the version used by the R.S.C.D.S. for the dance. It is not precisely correct to assign the tune to Niel Gow (as the Society has done); 'Niel Gow's set' would have been more accurate.

163

Speed the Plough

The tune *Speed the Plough*, a good reel, has been most popular in Scotland as well as the country dance which, incidentally, was also known as *Inverness Country Dance* in some places. The tune was composed by John Morehead in 1800 and first called *The Naval Pillar*. In this same year, Thomas Morton's (*c*. 1764 - 1838) sentimental play with a rural setting, *Speed the Plough*, was produced in London, and here we have the source of the name for the tune and the dance. It seems reasonable to suggest that the tune changed its name by being used for the Country Dance named after the play, but there is no proof of this. The earliest printed version of the dance discovered so far is in Mozart Allan's *Ballroom Guide*, 1880, but the tune is found as *Speed the Plough* in the earlier half of the century.

The play is famous for the creation of that embodiment of English respectability, Mrs. Grundy, who although often referred to in the play, never actually appears in it.

The Stoorie Miller

This dance, I understand (its source is not disclosed), was originally entitled *The Dusty Miller*; but since there is already a dance of that name in the R.S.C.D.S. collection, the title was changed to *Stoorie Miller*. The Scots word 'stoor' being translated as 'dust in flight'.

Whatever the background to the figures, we have here a superb Country Dance. One of the best Strathspeys in the list. The principal tune selected for it, too, is in the first rank — Marshall's *Mrs. Lumsden of Achindores*. We need say no more.

Strip the Willow

This has long been a favourite party dance and remains, with the *Eightsome Reel* and *Gay Gordons*, staple fare at country hops all over the Highlands and Islands. It began life as a folk dance — a weaving dance — inspired by the movements of the loom, employing a running step to music in 9/8, and this is how the R.S.C.D.S. represents it. Popularly, however, it is performed to Irish single jigs, in 6/8, of which *The Muckin' o' Geordie's Byre* is widely

164

favoured. It is certainly enjoyable to perform this dance to single jigs, in which case the travelling step should be a chasé (as used in quadrilles). Unfortunately, the character of the dance, with its series of turns, invites among the inept, or irresponsible, a wild spinning and throwing about of the ladies and crude stamping and hopping instead of the controlled chasé and deportment which makes the dance a work of art. There are some young women who actually enjoy being subjected to the rough house of whirling and slinging, but they are a small minority. In any case, such antics cannot be called dancing and represents all that the enthusiastic country dancer abhors.

Curiously enough, *Strip the Willow* in its authentic folk form, in 9/8, cannot be other than decorous — except insofar as the running step is not easy to perform elegantly — and no doubt that is why it finds its way into the R.S.C.D.S. repertoire. Although, as a 9/8 folk dance, it is never going to achieve much favour in the ballroom.

The Souters o' Selkirk

The 'souters' — shoemakers — of Selkirk, a Border town. Another word for souter was 'cordiner'.

Tytler, the eighteenth century antiquarian and historian, wrote of the ballad of this name:

> This ballad is founded on the following incident: Previous to the battle of Flodden, the town-clerk of Selkirk conducted a band of eighty *souters*, or shoemakers of that town, who joined the army; and the town-clerk in reward of his loyalty, was created a knight banneret by that prince [James IV]. They fought gallantly, and most of them were cut off. A few who escaped, found, on their return, in the forest of Ladywood edge, the wife of one of their brethren lying dead, and her child sucking her breast. Thence the town of Selkirk obtained for their arms, a woman sitting upon a sarcophagus, holding a child in her arms; in the back ground a wood; and on the sarcophagus the arms of Scotland.

Another authority of the same period, Ritson, points out that the idea that the souters of Selkirk could amount to eighty in 1513 is utterly incredible; but this is disputable (cf. Scott's *Minstrelsy*).

That Selkirk men did participate in the battle of Flodden and that the town 'and inhabitants thairof, continualie sen the Field of

165

Flodoune has been oppressit, heriit and owre run be theves and traitors, whairthrow the hant of merchandice has cessit amangis thame of langtyme bygane . . .' there is no doubt. It was in recognition of this that James V bestowed on Selkirk the status and privileges of a royal burgh in June 1536.

Stenhouse writes that the appellation 'Souters' is given to the burgesses of Selkirk, whether shoemakers or not: 'and appears to have originated from the singular custom observed at the admission of a new member, a ceremony which is on no account dispensed with. Some hog-bristles are attached to the seal of his burgess ticket; these he must dip in wine, and pass between his lips, as a tribute of his respect to this ancient and useful fraternity.'

Mr. Robertson, the minister of Selkirk, in his statistical account of the parish, declares that the ballad was written 'to commemorate a game of football between the shoemakers of Selkirk and the men of Hume'. But Sir Walter Scott discounts this; and although Robertson is correct in stating that the Earldom of Hume — mentioned in the best-known version of the ballad — did not exist at the time of Flodden, there was a Lord Hume (or 'Home') who played a controversial part in that battle.

Indeed, Lord Hume was warden of the eastern marches at the time and some time before Flodden had made a foray into England with 8000 men which led to his being ambushed at a pass called Broomhouse with considerable loss.

The causes or purposes of the attack on England by James IV are too involved for treatment here. One thing is clear, it was tragically unnecessary and to no useful purpose. Even if the Scots had been victorious, what would it have done but draw the redoubled fury of Henry VIII upon them just when his hands were freed in France. Of course, this was just it. Henry was occupied in a quarrel with France and James was persuaded to ease the pressure on his auld ally by attacking the auld enemy, even if Henry was his brother-in-law.

The Scots were overwhelmed at Flodden, drawn from a position of strength by guile and cut down by superior armament. James IV was last of the Scottish Kings to subscribe to the chivalric code of a slightly earlier age and he was too 'froward' in battle, not an ideal commander.

The battle was a major disaster for Scotland, the carnage terrible. Hardly a noble house but lost some flower of knighthood. The king himself falling in the field, leaving his nation a prey to the rapacity of its predominant barons, his son being but a child.

I've heard them liltan at the ewe milkan,
Lassie's a liltan at break of day,
But now they are groanan on ilka green loanin'
The floo'rs o' the forest are a' wede awa.

The Scottish renaissance was stillborn, the losses at Flodden saw to that. In a way, one can say that Scotland never really recovered.

At the battle, Lord Hume led the first charge — on the English right wing under Sir Edmund Howard — and routed his opponents. His Borderers then halted to secure prisoners and loot the English baggage-wagons on to which their adversaries had retreated and inadvertently led them out of sight of the main battle. Hume could not or did not re-form his men in time to participate further in the battle, and it is for this that he was widely criticized.

Nevertheless, Hume covered the withdrawal from the field and the English were by no means certain that theirs was the victory.

But the king and almost all his leaders had fallen.

Still from the sire the son shall hear
Of the stern strife, and carnage drear,
    Of Flodden's fatal field,
Where shiver'd was fair Scotland's spear,
    And broken was her shield.

SCOTT — *Marmion*

But it's,

Up wi' the Souters o' Selkirk,
And down wi' the fazart Lord Hume,
But up wi' ilka braw callant
That sews the single-soled shoon;
And up wi' the lads o' the Forest,
That ne'er to the Southron wad yield,
But deil scoup o' Hume and his menzie,
That stood sae abiegh on the field.

Fie! on the green and the yellow,
The crawhearted loons o' the Merse;
But here's tae the Souters o' Selkirk,
The elshin, the lingle, and birse.
Then up wi' the Souters o' Selkirk,
For they are baith trusty and leil;
And up wi' the lads o' the forest —
And down wi' the Merse to the deil.

The tune *The Souters o' Selkirk*, being a 3/2 hornpipe, is unsuitable for Scottish Country Dance technique, and consequently a Reel tune has been used by the R.S.C.D.S.

167

Struan Robertson

— Or Robertson of Strowan, chief of Clan Robertson (or Donnachaidh, in Gaelic). The estate of Strowan is adjacent to that of the Duke of Atholl in Perthshire. The Struan Robertson commemorated by the rant and by the Country Dance would be Alexander Robertson of Strowan who repeatedly put himself and family to hazard in the Jacobite cause during his long life (1670-1749). He joined Bonnie Dundee as a youth in 1688, as a result of which the family estate to which he had but recently fallen heir was forfeited to the crown. He retired in consequence to the court of the exiled King James at St. Germains during which time he served in two campaigns in the French army, a dramatic extreme for one who had been sent to the University of St. Andrews destined for the church. Queen Anne granted him a remission in 1703, whereupon he returned to Scotland only to join the Earl of Mar with about 500 of his clan in the unsuccessful rebellion of 1715. He was taken prisoner at Sheriffmuir but was rescued; then a little later fell into the hands of Government soldiers who conducted him to Edinburgh. Once again he was rescued, this time by his sister Margaret, who helped him escape to France. The estate of Strowan was granted to her, but she bequeathed it to her brother. Thus upon her death in 1727, he fell heir to his own property. The political climate was such that he received a remission for life in 1731, which enabled him to return to Scotland and take possession of his lands. As if he had not endured enough he marshalled support for Prince Charlie in 1745 but this time he was protected from his zeal by the infirmities of age. He died in his house of Carie in Rannoch without lawful issue and in him ended the direct male line of the Robertsons of Strowan reaching back to King Malcolm III. He left a collection of poems in English along with a history of the martial achievements of his family and is believed to have provided the prototype of the Baron of Bradwardine in Sir Walter Scott's Jacobite novel *Waverley*. He was certainly worthy of a tune and a dance.

The Theekit Hoose

The Theekit ('thatched') Hoose gives us an excuse to pass a word or two on the subject of Scotland's 'wee hooses in the heather' and other characteristic domestic dwellings of Highlands and Lowlands in years past.

As in every age and with every nation, the comfort and commodiousness of the houses of the population varied with the means or quality of the indivual occupants. Perhaps it is true that some Scottish lairds in, say, the seventeenth century, did not live in premises which were very much superior to those of their tenant farmers; but it is certain that, in time, distinctions increased. The nobility, of course, built fortified houses — or 'castles' — then later resorted to unfortified mansion houses.

In the seventeenth century most town houses were still built of wood and roofed with thatch. Two-storey dwellings were usually constructed of stone in the lower floor and wood, or wooden frontage, in the upper floor. The danger from fire became increasingly serious as the burghs grew in size. Catastrophic fires affected Dunfermline (1624), Glasgow (1652) and Kilmarnock (1668), for instance. Glasgow, in those days, was more comparable to Dunfermline and Kilmarnock than it is to-day. One thousand families were left homeless in Glasgow. In the locality of Briggait, Gallowgate and Saltmarket, the tenements associated with eighty closes were destroyed. The chaos caused was shocking and a general collection was hastily conducted throughout the kingdom to provide relief.

We can well appreciate the gravity of the problem in a city like Edinburgh with its tall 'lands' and congestion on the rock. Thus it comes as no surprise to note the initiative being taken there in 1677 to ensure that all new construction would be in stone and all new roofs of 'sclaitt and tyll'.

In the countryside we are tempted to distinguish between Highland and Lowland in the matter of house construction; but the similarities were greater than the differences. Certainly the low, thick-walled, thatched, 'black' house of the West Highlands and Islands survived longer in its original state than the same kind of dwelling in the Lowlands. Survived, indeed, right into the present century. The Hebridean 'black-house' differed from its Lowland counterpart in such matters as shape — it was not rectangular — and internal appointments. Wood, of course, was very scarce on the islands, and this was reflected in the furnishings. Beds were sometimes recessed into the outside walls, which were usually five to six feet thick, or constructed of a framework of rough laths covered with straw and sheltered from leaks through the roof by a canopy of 'divots' (turfs) supported by four upright posts, a 'four-poster' indeed.

The corresponding mainland structure was rectangular in shape and built of the same loose undressed stones, walls not quite so thick, and about four to five feet in height. The spaces between the stones were filled with clay or divots. The rafters were set in the walls and rose to an apex of about eight or nine feet. These were joined by purlins and laid over with rough boughs which formed a framework for a roof covering of turf or a thatch of rushes, fern, or heather fastened down by straw ropes. The over-hanging thatch was not so far from the ground that the hens could not venture upon it and scrape for food, and rats, too, could get into it as Burns — who was very familiar with such a house — remarks:

> There, lanely by the ingle-cheek
> I sat and ey'd the spewing reek,
> That fill'd wi' hoast-provoking smeek
> The auld clay biggin;
> An' heard the restless rattons squeak
> About the riggin'.

The Vision

('ingle-cheek' — fireside; 'hoast' -- cough; 'rattons' — rats)

The house was filled with smoke because chimneys were not a common feature until the nineteenth century in houses of this kind. The reason is not very clear. In the Hebridean black-house, straw thatch was used, which soon became well impregnated with soot. This provided a valuable manure.

The smoke then, in both classes of house, permeated every-thing and found its way out at the low door or by a hole serving as a window. The fire was built in a circle of stones, usually in the centre of the room, and often hens shared the warmth, roosting on the 'cabars' or beams. The floor was earthen or of packed clay and ash.

In both Highlands and Lowlands the cows, oxen or horses, shared the same accommodation, separated from the human habitation by a wattled partition, or in the Hebrides, a kerb of stones.

Of course, not all people were farmers, but even the weaver or 'soutar' or ferryman would have a cow very often.

On the mainland, the typical house comprised three apart-ments – the cowhouse or 'byre', the kitchen or living-room, and an inner apartment called the 'spence'. Animals and tenants entered by the same door, but the animals would turn one way and the humans the other into the byre and kitchen respectively. The byre was sometimes separated from the kitchen by a passage which ran from front to rear of the house, having a door at either end — the 'through-gang'. The kitchen, or living-room, was the central apartment and between that and the gable was the 'spence' a kind of small 'drawing room' for receiving particular guests, or to which master or mistress could retire for a measure of privacy and store important belongings, meal chest, spinning wheel and sowens tub.

Box-beds were used, that is beds enclosed in wooden cabinets fitted with sliding doors. Very often the roof cross beams were floored with brushwood and divots and an attic apartment formed there for extra sleeping accommodation. The other furnishings were simple — wooden dresser, shelves, complete with a bright array of pewter trenchers, bowls, plates, spoons or 'luggies', 'mutchkins', 'stoups', 'tassies', 'coggies' and 'bickers' and the like.

Cottages built on this plan were said to consist of a *butt* and *ben*, and this term 'butt and ben' remains in the language as a name for a two-roomed house. To go 'ben' means, still, to enter the living quarters of a house.

In the early part of the eighteenth century, there still survived some much more primitive dwellings built mostly of turf or of mud plastered on lattice work; but these were not typical. That the inferior sort of *butt and ben* was going out by the 1790's seems to be indicated by Robert Heron, who had occasion to enter one during his tour of the Highlands in the Autumn of 1792. He had just been ferried across the Tummel at Logierait and, desiring to refresh himself and his horses, called at the boatman's house. It exhibited, he writes, 'a scene of nastiness and simplicity which convinced me that the primitive manners of my country were not everywhere lost'. His description illustrates the worst features of some of the details mentioned above:

It was a low, smoky hut, the door of which could hardly be entered without creeping. The thatched roof was not rainproof; and all the rafters were dropping an inky fluid. On each side of the door, a partition ran through the house: it was formed of stakes driven into the ground, interwoven with twigs, or willow-branches, and the whole plastered, on both sides, with clay. . . . One end of the house was appropriated to the purposes of a bed-room, store-room, cellar, pantry, and apartment for the accommodation of strangers (the 'spence'). It were hard to say whether dampness, dirt, or disorder seemed to predominate most in it. The other was the kitchen; and into it I entered. Here was a smoking fire in the middle of the floor. I am not sure whether or not there might be a hole in the roof for

171

the discharge of smoke. If there was, it was certainly inadequate for the purpose; for the smoke was diffused through the kitchen, so as to obscure it with almost palpable darkness. Immediately around the fire was a small sphere within which the darkness was visible. Here sat the mistress of the family with several of her children beside her. The good woman was dirty, black and overgrown, and seemed just Sir John Falstaff in petticoats. The children were half-naked and dirty, but with health and cheerfulness in their looks. They conversed together in Gaelic. I addressed the mother. She could speak a little, and but a very little broken English; the children neither spoke nor understood a syllable of English. In compliance with my request, the good woman soon produced her whisky bottle, with bread and cheese. . . .The scene was simple as the hut of a savage; there was the same squalid nastiness, the same aspect of vigorous health, and the same cheerful, kind hospitality; as society is said to present in its simplest and rudest forms. I was, in consequence, more gratified than I should have been in a more commodious inn, and with better entertainment.'

A short time later, near Killin, the same writer comments on 'little houses well built of stone and lime' and well-thatched, which reveals the trend of progress already well advanced. The Scottish cottage remained basically of the same form, but it now moved in the direction of larger and glazed windows, wooden or tiled floors, whitewashed outer walls and even of finished stone and lime. The animals and the *midden* were moved away from the house and so on, and last of all came the slate roof and the theekit cottage was no more, although it is recalled well within living memory.

Before we allude disparagingly to the rude stone cottages and black houses of Scotland and use such words as 'squalid', 'wretched', 'shabby', 'dirty', 'oppressive' and so on; let us remind ourselves of what thinkers, musicians, scientists, engineers, explorers and poets were born in one, or something not far removed from one.

> But how it comes I never kent yet,
> They're maistly wonderfu' contented;
> An' buirdly chiels and clever hizzies
> Are bred in sic a way as this is.
>
> BURNS — *Twa Dugs*

There's Nae Luck aboot the Hoose

The authorship of this most durable and well-loved song is a matter of dispute — William Mickle of Langholm, or, more probably, Jean Adams (1710-65) a schoolmistress of Crawfordsdyke, Greenock, or neither. The evidence is inconclusive.

Burns wrote of it as follows: 'This is one of the most beautiful songs in the Scots or any other language. The two lines:

> And will I see his face again!
> And will I hear him speak?

as well as the two preceding ones, are unequalled almost by anything I ever heard or read: and the lines,

> The present moment is our ain
> The neist we never saw

are worthy of the first poet. It is long posterior to Ramsay's days. About the year 1771 or '72, it came first on the streets as a ballad; and I suppose the composition of the song was not much anterior to that period.'

There are seven substantial verses to the song. The first and last two are the strongest verses and well bear out Burns' opinion. Dr. Beattie, the famous eighteenth century divine, is vouched to have written the last verse. Here are these three verses:

And are ye sure the news is true?
And are ye sure he's weel?
Is this the time tae talk o' work
Mak haste! Set by your wheel.
Is this the time to talk o' work,
When Colin's at the door!
Gie me my cloak! I'll to the Quey
And see him come ashore.

Chorus:
For there's nae luck aboot the hoose,
There's nae luck ava;
There's little pleasure in the hoose,
When our guidman's awa.

The cauld blasts o' the winter wind
That thrilled thro' my heart.
They're blaen by, I hae him safe,
Till death we'll never part;
But what puts parting in my head?
It may be far awa,
The present moment is our ain;
The neist we never saw.

Since Colin's wed, I'm content,
I hae nae mair tae crave;
Could I but live to mak him blest,
I'm blest aboon the lave;
And will I see his face again
And will I hear him speak!
I'm downright dizzy wi' the thocht;
In troth I'm like to greet.

This is no my ain Hoose

The dance of this name, published by the R.S.C.D.S., was reconstructed from the so-called Holmain MSS. (1730-50), the source of a number of other good Country Dances. As usual, the dance originally took its name from the tune, one of a family of sets springing from the same source which were current at the end of the seventeenth century. An almost identical dance to the same tune is included in another MS. of about the same period compiled for the Duke of Perth. It has every appearance of being the same dance and may be of interest!

First crouple cross hands with the 2nd couple, and go quite round and cast off. Then cross hands with the 3rd couple and go round to the second couple's place, and cast off. Sett to your partner and turn half round improper. Then back to back, the first man cast round the 3rd woman, the first woman cast round the 2nd man till you come where you was. Back to back again, first man cast round the 2nd woman, the first woman go round the 3rd man. Sett across and turn. Then sett across again and turn your partner.

The tune to this dance in the MS. is recognizably the same as that given in the Crocket MS. (1709), but syncopated somewhat and less varied. It is best known by the name of its old verses:

O, this is no my ain hoose,
  My ain hoose, my ain hoose;
This is no my ain hoose,
  I ken by the biggin o't.

This is no my ain wean,
  My ain wean, my ain wean;
This is no my ain wean,
  I ken by the greetie o't.

The original tune, from which the other sets are thought to be derived is *De'il stick the Minister*. One of the best of them is *Seann Triubhas Willican*, or as Burns spelt it — *Shuan Truish Willighan* — a double hornpipe, and the original tune of the solo dance *Seann Triubhas* (now performed to *Whistle o'er the lave o't*). Burns, playing it '*largo-lento*', was attracted to it for a song of his own *I see a form, I see a face*, of which the chorus reveals its ancestry.

174

> This is no my ain lassie
> Fair tho' the lassie be;
> Weel ken I my ain lassie —
> Kind love is in her e'e.

Now, this tune played in this way falls into Strathspey treatment so beautifully that one would swear that it could not ever have been anything else. It therefore is somewhat annoying that the Society did not turn to this set of the old tune for the Country Dance. It is possible that the relationship was not known. However, the tunes selected for the dance by the Society are — *Mrs. Colonel Sinclair of Forss* and *Willie Shaw*, which have no particular history.

Weel may the dance say — 'This is no my ain tune, I ken by the diddle o't' !

Tibby Fowler o' the Glen

> Tibbie Fowler o' the Glen;
> There's ower mony wooing at her;
> Tibbie Fowler o' the Glen,
> There's ower mony wooing at her.
>
> Wooin' at her, pu'in' at her,
> Courtin' her, and canna get her;
> Filthy elf, it's for her pelf,
> That a' the lads are wooin' at her.

There are several verses to this humerous song on the cynical theme of money being of greater allurement than beauty. Tibby, apparently had 'penny siller' consequently:

> There's seven, but, and seven ben,
> Seven in the pantry wi' her;
> Twenty head about the door:
> There's ane-and-forty wooin' at her!
>
> Wooin' at her, etc.

Tradition identifies Tibby as Isabella Fowler of Burncastle, and the successful one of the 'ane-and-forty' as George Logan of Restalrig. Campbell writes in his *History of Leith*: 'We think it not improbable that it was tibbie's tocher that enabled Logan, who was ruined by the attainder of 1609, to build the elegant mansion on the Sherrif Brae'.

This house, long pointed out in Leith as that of Tibbie and her husband, was demolished in 1840 to make way for St. Thomas' Church.

Todlen Hame

Ramsay published words to this song and it is found set to two different tunes; one, the original in the *Orpheus Caledonius* (1733) and the other, sometimes known as *My ain fireside*, in Johnson's *Museum*.

> When I hae saxpence under my thoom,
> Then I get credit in ilka toun;
> But, aye when I'm puir they bid me gang by,
> Oh, poverty parts gude company!
>   Todlin' hame, todlin' hame,
>   Couldna my love come todlin' hame.

Tullochgorum

Tullochgorum is a district in the Aberdeenshire Highlands. The tune *The Reel of Tullochgorum* is in the Drummond Castle MS. (1734), and was a favourite tune, we can be sure, long before that time. The Reverend Mr. John Skinner (1721-1807) wrote verses for it and Burns in writing to Skinner praised the latter's poem as 'the best Scotch song ever Scotland saw'.

Burns, in his *Reliques*, tells us how it came to be written:

> This First of Songs is the masterpiece of my old friend Skinner. He was, I think passing the day at the town of Cullen; I think it was, in a friend's house, whose name was Montgomery. Mrs. Montgomery observing, en passant, that the beautiful reel of Tullochgorum wanted words; she begged them of Mr. Skinner, who gratified her wishes.'

The third of the six verses of this long-neglected, but once popular song, warrants inclusion here:

> What needs there be sae great a fraise
> Wi' dringing dull Italian lays,
> I wadna gie our ain Strathspeys
>   For half a hunder score o' them;
> They're dowf and dowie at the best,
>   Dowf and dowie, dowf and dowie,
>   Dowf and dowie at the best,
>   Wi' a' their variorum;
> They're dowf and dowie at the best,
> Their allegro's and a' the rest,
> They canna please a Scottish taste,
>   Compar'd wi' Tullochgorum.

Torryburn Lasses

Torryburn is a village near Dunfermline. The particular country dance bearing that name was collected by the R.S.C.D.S. in Perthshire. The tune from which it takes its title was originally called *Tadie's Wattle* and was re-named by Nat. Gow.

Triumph

The meaning of this dance is as follows:

> The first man leads his partner down with pride; but on the couple's return to the top, the lady disengages from her partner to accept the proffered left hand of the second man who then leads her down the dance with rapturous satisfaction; the first man trails behind with chagrin. At the bottom, the lady turns by the right and while leaving her right hand in the left hand of her new partner, capriciously extends her left hand across her body to her former partner who takes it in his right. The two men join their free hands in an arch behind the lady's head, and they, particularly the first man — and the lady — return in 'triumph'.

The tune, a very catchy hornpipe (4/4) was first published by Aird, the Glasgow music seller, in 1797. The dance was said to have been introduced to Scottish assemblies by Nathaniel Gow in 1808 and it and its tune certainly remained favourites in Scotland right into the twentieth century. Another variant of the dance was collected in the English countryside by Cecil Sharp's friends in the late nineteenth century.

Twenty-first of September

This was the date of the rout of Sir John Cope's army by the Jacobite highlanders at Prestonpans in 1745. The Jacobite army had moved from Edinburgh, of which it had taken possession, intent on engaging Cope's forces hurriedly mustered after their disembarkation at Dunbar on the nineteenth. For a few days prior to that two companies of dragoons had waited at Prestonpans with such apprehension that, on the night of the sixteenth, when a dragoon fell into an open coal pit with a great clangour of side arms and accoutrements, they fled in panic. We have this story from Alexander Carlyle who goes on to tell us:

> Before six on Tuesday morning, the 17th, Mr. James Hey, a gentleman in the town. . . came to my bedside, and eagerly enquired what I thought was to be done, as the dragoons, in marching along in their confusion had strewed the road eastward with accoutrements of every kind — pistols, swords, skullcaps, etc. I said that people should be employed immediately to gather them up, and send them after, and this was done, and amounted to what filled a close cart and a couple of creels on horseback.

178

Cope took up a good defensive position at Prestonpans, separated from the Jacobite forces by a marsh. Both armies were about 2000 strong, but only about 1500 of Prince Charlie's men had both swords and muskets, about another hundred had scythes fastened to poles and the remainder made do with sticks. Unfortunately for Cope, the proprietor of the marshy ground was favourably disposed to the Jacobites and revealed to them a passage across it. Through this the Highlanders defiled stealthily, shortly before the dawn revealed their new position. Cope had little time to recover from his surprise before the first line of Highlanders, Lord George Murray at their head, charged, sword in hand, upon the encampment.

In the words of an anti-Jacobite observer: 'They came on with furious precipitation. . .and it may be fittly called the Chase of Cockenie or Tranent reither than the battell, for never deers run faster befor hounds than these poor betrayed men ran befor a rabbell. . . .They were surprised in the twelight by men came on with a resolut rage.' [Woodhouslee MS]

> Hey Johnie Cope are ye waukin' yet
> And are y'r drums abeatin' yet. . .

The Country Dance is derived from Wm. Campbell's collection (c. 1796) and indeed suggests something of the confusion and action of the occasion commemorated by its title.

Up in the Air

The only verses extant of this song are by Alan Ramsay. It is a bacchanalian song with a light mystical touch, so characteristic of Hogg in a certain strain and so uncharacteristic of Lowland song in general; but fascinating in its effect. The word 'Celtic' comes to one's tongue. The imagination, liberated by the potent glass, leaps into the frosty night while the flesh warms in the glow of both fire and liquid spirit.

Now the sun's gane out of sight,
  Beet the ingle, and snuff the light.
In glens the fairies skip and dance,
And witches wallop o'er to France.
  Up in the air, on my bonny grey mare,
And I see her yet, and I see her yet.

The wind's drifting hail and sna',
  Oer frozen hags, like a foot-ba';
Nae starns keek thro' the azure slit,
'Tis cauld and mirk as ony pit.
  The man i' the moon is carousing aboon,
D'ye see, d'ye see, d'ye see him yet?

179

This, then, is Ramsay's framework for the old tune; but the R.S.C.D.S. has used another tune for the dance — *Sir George Clark of Pennycuik*, a Strathspey. There is a sentimental link here which one would like to think was intentional; Alan Ramsay was a close friend of that family in his time and set his 'Gentle Shepherd' in their locality, the valley of the Tweed near the Pentland Hills. He also dedicated this poem to Susanna, Countess of Eglintoun, who was at one time an object of Sir John Clerk's admiration; Sir John being an ancestor of Sir George whose name is preserved by our tune.

Sir John's lines to Susanna were worthy of a better response. He wrote them on a piece of paper and rolled it inside a flute which he sent her as a gift:

Harmonious pipe, how I envy thy bliss,
When press'd to Sylphia's lips with gentle kiss!
And when her tender fingers round thee move
In soft embrace, I listen and approve
Those melting notes, which soothe my soul to love.
Embalm'd with odours from her breath that flow,
You yield your music when she's pleased to blow;
And thus at once the charming lovely fair
Delights with sounds, with sweets perfumes the air.
Go happy pipe, and ever mindful be
To court the charming Sylphia for me:
Tell all I feel — you cannot tell too much —
Repeat my love at each soft melting touch;
Since I to her my liberty resign,
Take then the care to tune her heart to mine.

The Village Reel

The original dance was probably set to a Reel from *Love in a Village*, published by Stewart in the 1760's. The Country Dance was culled by the R.S.C.D.S. from one of Campbell's publications (1794). The ballad opera *Love in a Village* was written by Isaac Bickerstaffe the popular Irish playwright of the second half of the eighteenth century. Another of his 'musicals' was *Maid of the Mill*.

West's Hornpipe

The original dance in *The Ladies Pocket Book* (1797) was, of course, to that tune called *West's Hornpipe*. The R.S.C.D.S., however, preferred another principal tune for the dance — *Robertson's Hornpipe* — but retained the original title as though it belonged to the figures. West was a stage dancer.

The White Cockade

This excellent Scottish Measure was formerly called *The Ranting Highlandman*, that is, before Burns took a fancy to it. The original words, in Herd:

My love was born in Aberdeen
The bonniest lad that e'er was seen;
O he is forced frae me to gae
Over the hills and far away.

Burns changed it into a Jacobite song:

My love was born in Aberdeen,
The bonniest lad that e'er was seen,
But now he makes our hearts fu' sad,
He takes the field wi' his White Cockade.
O he's a ranting, roving lad,
He is a brisk an' a bonny lad,
Betide what may, I will be wed,
And follow the boy wi' the White Cockade.

The white rosette (cockade) was chosen as the emblem of the Jacobites in contradistinction to the black rosette of the Hanoverians.

Another song by Burns — 'A highland lad my love was born', from his *Jolly Beggars* cantata — is often sung to this tune, although it was originally set to another excellent Scottish Measure — *O an ye were dead gudeman* which some may know as the tune of *There was a lad was born in Kyle*; although here again we have an 'adoption', it did not originally belong to this song.

181

She turn'd, and she blush'd, and she smil'd,
 And she lookit sae bashfully doun;
The pride o' her hert was beguiled,
 And she play'd wi' the sleeve o' her goun,
She twirl'd the tag o' her lace,
 And she nippit her boddice sae blue,
Syne blinket sae sweet in his face,
 And aff like a mawkin she flew.

Woo'd and married and a',
Married and carried awa';
She thinks hersel' very weel aff,
 To be woo'd and married an a'.

The tune to this song is a 9/8 jig and the dance published by the R.S.C.D.S. is taken from Wilson's *Ballroom Companion* (1816). Irish steps — 'hop jig' — were requisite for 9/8 tunes in Wilson's time; but this rhythm is not used in Scottish Country Dancing today. Hence the dance is now set to a 6/8 jig.

Ye'll aye be Welcome Back Again

At first glance a Jacobite title, and of course it could be used as an allusion to Prince Charlie, but it does not belong to a Jacobite song. The original verses are somewhat bawdy (cf. Burns' *Merry Muses*), at least the verses which survived to reach the printed page. The tune is also known as *Duncan Davidson*, and it first appears in print in John Walsh's *Caledonian Country Dances*.
The moral of the song is in the last four lines:

A man may drink, and no be drunk;
A man may fight, and no be slain;
A man may kiss a bonnie lass,
And aye be welcome back again!

The Yellow-Haired Laddie

This is one of the more beautiful airs of Scottish song but, since it is in slow triple time, it is of the character of a Minuet as far as dance rhythm is concerned and thus, with *Tweedside*, is somewhat anomalous in a collection of Scottish Country Dances. Of course, Country Dances were not restricted to 6/8 jigs, common-time hornpipes and reels and Strathspeys in eighteenth century Scottish dancing circles. Some were also in the rhythms associated with 3/2 and 9/8. But these were clearly not suitable for the strong indigenous tradition of step technique which is the peculiarly Scottish contribution to the form.

However, the song *Yellow-haired laddie* is not about Prince Charlie as is often assumed. Ramsay published the old words in 1724 and wrote two sets of his own. Somehow none of these are worthy of the tune. The original carries more true feeling:

> The yellow-hair'd laddie sat down on yon brae,
>   Cries, milk the ewes, lassie, let nane o them gae,
> And aye she milked, and aye she sang,
> The yellow-hair'd laddie shall be my goodman.
>   And aye she milked, etc.
>
> The weather is cauld, and my claithing is thin,
> The ewes are new clipped, they winna bught in;
> They winna bught in tho' I shou'd die,
> O yellow-hair'd laddie, be kind to me,
>   They winna bught in, etc.
>
> The goodwife cries butt the house, Jenny, come ben,
> The cheese is to mak, and the butter's to kirn;
> Tho' butter, and cheese, and a' shou'd flowre,
> I'll crack and kiss wi' my love ae half hour;
> It's ae half hour, and we's e'en mak it three,
> For the yellow-hair'd laddie my husband shall be.

Ramsay's versions begin:

(1)   In April, when primroses paint the sweet plain,

and

(2)   When first my dear laddie gaed to the green hill.

185

Y're Welcome, Charlie Stewart

The story is told that on the anniversary of the Battle of Culloden, some English officers in the dress circle of the Canongate Theatre, Edinburgh, called on the orchestra to play *Culloden*, a jig which is not very well known to-day. This was resented by the audience who retaliated by demanding *Y're welcome, Charlie Stewart*. Something akin to a riot developed and, we can have no doubt, the officers would be glad to beat a retreat. The tune was originally known as *Miss Stewart's Reel*, the Jacobite verses were attached to it in the year 1748. Then Burns used the tune for two songs on friends of his — *Lovely Polly Stewart* and *Y're welcome, Willie Stewart*.

Auld Lang Syne and *Gude Nicht and Joy be wi' ye a'*

It has been a strange and exciting fate for an old Scottish lyric to become the best-known song in the world. It has, indeed, penetrated to every corner of the globe to which Scots have ventured, serving as a fitting finale for every festive gathering. Since the most popular occasion in the Scots calendar is the welcome of the New Year, even those who are not Scots have come to adopt *Auld Lang Syne* as a special New Year song.

It is a song of old friendship, ennobled by the sincerity and strength of its simple expression.

Should auld acquaintance be forgot,
And never brought to min'?
Should auld acquaintance be forgot,
And days o' lang syne?

Chorus:
For auld lang syne, my dear,
For auld lang syne;
We'll tak a cup o' kindness yet,
For auld lang syne.

We twa ha'e run about the braes,
And pu'd the gowans[1] fine;
But we've wandered many a weary fit,
Sin' auld lang syne.

We twa ha'e paid'lt in the burn,
Frae morning sun till dine;
But seas between us braid ha'e roar'd
Sin' auld lang syne.

And there's a hand, my trusty fere[2]
And gi'es a haun o' thine;
And we'll tak a richt-gude-willie waught[3]
For auld lang syne.

And surely ye'll be your pint stoup,
And surely I'll be mine;
And we'll tak' a cup o' kindness yet
For auld lang syne.

[1] Daisies.   [2] Friend.   [3] A draught with right good will.

The first, second and third of the above verses and partially the chorus are recreations by Robert Burns, the remainder are from the original which the poet tells us he obtained from the singing of an old man. In a letter to his friend Mrs. Dunlop he rhapsodies — 'Light be the turf on the breast of the heaven-inspired Poet who composed this glorious fragment! There is more of the fire of native genius in it, than in half a dozen of modern English Bacchanalians.'

The tune associated with the original words was in Burns' opinion 'mediocre', thus in Thomson's *Scots Airs* it was set to its present popular melody, a favourite Strathspey air which was first printed in Bremner's *Scots Reels* (1759) entitled *The Miller's Wedding*. Sets of the tune appear in later collections and is best known as *Sir Alexander Don's Strathspey* from its publication by Gow under that title in 1788. Sets of the tune were used for the well-known songs *O can ye labor lea* and *Comin' thro' the rye* in Johnson's *Musical Museum*.

The more universal use of *Auld Lang Syne* has led to some alterations and corruptions in the verses and, in any case, there is no need for more than two verses and chorus when it is used as a closing song. The accepted practice now is for the company to stand in a ring holding hands as they sing the first verse and chorus. Then follows the second last verse — "And there's a hand, my trusty fere' — on which line, hands are released and re-clasped with the arms crossing in front of the body and moving up and down in a shaking motion in time to the music. Then, on the chorus, the hands remaining clasped, all walk, or dance, towards the centre and out again to complete the ritual.

The use of *Auld Lang Syne* in this way dates from the early nineteenth century. Prior to that time it was customary for the musicians to play or the company to sing the lively Scottish Measure *Gude Night and Joy be wi' ye a'* at the close of every convivial evening.

This tune appears in an early seventeenth century MS. (the *Skene*) and has had several sets of verses written for it by distinguished eighteenth century song writers, such as Joanna Baillie, James Hogg and Sir Alex. Boswell, James Boswell's son. Burns instructed Johnson as follows: 'Let this be your last song in all the collection and set it to the old words'. He also asked him to append his own verses to the air. The old words, sometimes attributed to the Border freebooter, Johnny Armstrong (*c.* 1600), run as follows:

> The night is my departing night,
> The morn's the day I maun awa';
> There's no a friend or foe o' mine
> But wishes that I were awa'.
> What I hae done, for lake o' wit,
> I never, never can reca';
> I trust ye're a' my friends as yet,
> Gude night and joy be wi' you a'.

INDEX OF THE DANCES